T0346653

BEIRUT 1958

BEIRUT 1958

*How America's Wars
in the Middle East Began*

Bruce Riedel

Brookings Institution Press
Washington, D.C.

The Brookings Institution is a private nonprofit organization de-
voted to research, education, and publication on important issues
of domestic and foreign policy. Its principal purpose is to bring the
highest quality independent research and analysis to bear on current and emerging policy problems. Interpretations or conclusions
in Brookings publications should be understood to be solely those
of the authors.

Library of Congress Cataloging-in-Publication data are available.

ISBN 978-0-8157-3729-2 (hc)
ISBN 978-0-8157-3735-3 (ebook)

9 8 7 6 5 4 3 2 1

Composition by Elliott Beard

In loving memory of Alison Riedel

Contents

INTRODUCTION

On July 15, 1958, United States Marines stormed ashore at Beirut, Lebanon. It was the first ever American combat mission in the Middle East. The Marines were assaulting the beach in Beirut to prevent the spread of international communism, according to President Dwight David Eisenhower, who spoke to the nation that day.

I was there, only five years old. My father, who had served in the U.S. Army in Algeria and Italy during World War II, was working for the United Nations. Our family had accompanied him from our previous post in Jerusalem to Beirut. The assignment began as a joy—Beirut was then known as the Paris of the Middle East—but by July it was in the midst of a deadly civil war. According to what my parents later told me, we came under sniper fire more than once.

For the Marines it was a much more dangerous mission. Offshore the U.S. Navy had more than seventy warships deployed to back them up, including three aircraft carriers. In Germany, the U.S. Army was preparing to deploy to the beachhead a battalion of Honest John rocket launchers equipped with tactical nuclear weapons. Thankfully cooler minds prevailed, and the nukes never arrived.

The Beirut landing came amid a complex regional crisis that had been developing since the beginning of the year, when Egypt and Syria had united. A failed Saudi-backed coup in Damascus led to the sidelining of America's favorite Arab, King Saud. The Central Intelligence Agency foiled an Egyptian-backed coup in Jordan. Then on July 14, a coup ousted the most pro-Western leader in the region, King Faisal II in Iraq. Eisenhower, usually a very cool decisionmaker, panicked and sent the Marines into Beirut while the British intervened in Jordan.

An American combat military mission in the Middle East was a novelty in 1958. Americans had served in the region, in Iran and other places, during World War II but in logistical roles, helping to get supplies to our allies, including the Soviet Union. America also had built airbases for the U.S. Air Force, including one in Dhahran, Saudi Arabia, but they did not engage in combat operations. Beirut was a first.

Six decades later American combat operations in the Middle East are no longer a novelty; they are a constant. Indeed, America seems fated to never-ending wars in the

Middle East. American troops have fought in virtually every Middle Eastern country or supported combat operations from within them. The men and women of the U.S. armed forces have given the last full measure of devotion to their country, from Lebanon to Iraq to Yemen to Iran and so on. Their country owes them a debt of gratitude it can never pay.

Some of the combat missions have been absolutely necessary. The defense of Saudi Arabia from Saddam Hussein in 1990 certainly fits that category. Missions to kill or capture terrorists in the years since 9/11 also have been crucial to the defense of the United States.

But others have been ill-conceived. The deployment of American Marines to Beirut the second time, in 1982, was a poorly thought through peacekeeping mission that turned into disaster for the Marines when a terrorist truck bomb killed 241 soldiers. The second war with Iraq, in 2003, was another disaster, perhaps among the worst foreign policy mistakes in American history.

I have been involved in one way or another with most of these missions; first as an analyst at the Central Intelligence Agency (CIA) following the Iranian revolution and Israel's invasion of Lebanon, then on assignment in the Middle East collecting intelligence, then as the deputy director of the Persian Gulf Task Force during Operations Desert Shield and Desert Storm. I moved on to work in the White House for four presidents as an adviser on the wars in the region as well as on our efforts to promote peace.

I finished my career in the government assigned to the North Atlantic Treaty Organization (NATO) headquarters in Brussels closely following the Iraq war.

At the Brookings Institution, I have written and lectured extensively about America's wars in the Middle East. In this book I go back to how it began, to the first mission in Lebanon. This book tells the history of how Ike decided to send the Marines to Beirut, how that mission narrowly avoided becoming a quagmire, and how it ended with only one American killed in combat. At the Iwo Jima monument to the Marine Corps, overlooking Washington, D.C., "Lebanon 1958" is one of the Corps' battles inscribed on the base of the statue. How the Marines got to Lebanon is a fascinating tale of espionage and diplomacy filled with a colorful cast of characters.

I also describe a couple of lessons learned from this first combat mission and how it unfolded that may be useful to future policymakers confronting the challenge of future wars in the Middle East. And there are, indeed, some important lessons to be learned. The Middle East will always provide surprises and unexpected developments; it is always smart to avoid a rush to judgment when they suddenly happen.

My colleagues at Brookings were very helpful with their time and expertise in reviewing this book. My research assistant Israa Saber was particularly helpful in tracking down manuscripts and documents. As always, the Brookings library staff and Brookings Institution Press have been joys to work with. I also benefited from assistance from the Eisenhower Presidential Library and the Eisenhower Farm in Gettysburg, the Office of the Historian at the State Department, and the CIA's Electronic Reading Room. The CIA published an early version of the Saudi coup plot in Syria in its in-house journal *Studies in Intelligence.* I have been fascinated by the events of 1958 for decades, and countless Americans and Arabs have given me their insights. My wife Elizabeth traveled with me on this journey into the past and made it joyful.

This book was reviewed by the CIA prior to its publication. This does not constitute an official release of CIA information. All statements of fact, opinion, or analysis expressed are those of the author and do not reflect the official positions or views of the Central Intelligence Agency or any other U.S. government agency. Nothing in the contents should be construed as asserting or implying U.S. government authentication of information or CIA endorsement of the author's views. This material has been reviewed solely for classification.

One

JERUSALEM AND CAIRO

Gamal abd al Nasser! Gamal abd al Nasser! GAMAL ABD AL NASSER! The crowd marching down the road in front of our house in the Shaykh Jarrah neighborhood in Jerusalem rhythmically chanted the name of their handsome thirty-seven-year-old hero. The Egyptian president was the most revered man in East Jerusalem, the man Palestinians believed would deliver them from their misfortunes and unite the Arab world from "the ocean to the gulf." Americans, on the other hand, had already begun to vilify the Egyptian leader as a pro-Soviet revolutionary and enemy of the West.

Jordan in December 1955 was at the center of the storm about Nasser. Only seven years earlier it had annexed the West Bank and East Jerusalem to Transjordan and created the Hashemite Kingdom of Jordan. Its twenty-year-old king Hussein bin Talal had ascended to the throne less than three years before. The country was dependent on aid from the United Kingdom, which provided the leadership for its army. It was under pressure from the United Kingdom and the United States to align itself with a pro-Western alliance called the Baghdad Pact, which united Turkey, Iraq, Pakistan, and Iran with the West against the Soviet Union and its allies. Britain was at the head of the Baghdad Pact; it had organized its creation. The United States was a partner but preferred to let England take the lead in the Middle East and was not a formal treaty member. Among many Jordanians the Baghdad Pact was seen as an imperialist and reactionary *entente* intended to stifle Egypt and its charismatic leader.

Jerusalem had been a divided city since 1948. Jordan controlled the east while Israel controlled the west. Jordan held the old city where three religions had sacred sites: the Western Wall for the Jews, the Church of the Holy Sepulcher for the Christians, and the Dome of the Rock for the Muslims. Travel across the armistice line was prohibited except for a few individuals. My family was among the few allowed access, since my father worked for the United Nations Truce Supervision Organization, which monitored the armistice. We were allowed to drive back and forth through the Mandelbaum Gate, which was the opening in the lines.

The riots that broke out in Jordan on December 16, 1955, followed a visit to the country by the British Chief of the Imperial General Staff, General Sir Gerald Templer,

Gamal Abd al Nasser, Egypt's president
and America's nemesis.

whose mission was to "push Jordan over the brink" into joining the Baghdad Pact. He offered the young king an increase in financial aid and the honorary title of Air Vice Marshal in the Royal Air Force to sweeten the deal.[1] Templer was a hard man with little sense of nuance or decorum. His timing was also bad; Nasser had just sent his loyal lieutenant Anwar Sadat to urge the king to reject the pact, and Jordanians had cheered this hero of the Egyptian revolution.[2] "By all accounts, the Templer mission was a complete failure," notes one expert.[3]

The Baghdad Pact riots shook the fragile foundations of the Hashemite Kingdom and were the worst in Jordan's history. The entire country was engulfed. The worst unrest was in the Palestinian cities and towns of the West Bank, including East Jerusalem, but violence also broke out in the East Bank. Even in remote Aqaba on the Red Sea a mob sacked the American Point Four aid depot. In Jerusalem the consulates of the pact countries were attacked and the French and Turkish consuls wounded. In the capital, Amman, a general strike was declared.[4]

The king was so shaken by the riots that he asked his cousin, King Faisal II of Iraq, to prepare to send a division of troops to Jordan to help quell the unrest. The British quickly deployed two battalions of paratroopers and a battalion of Highland infantry to Cyprus, still a British colony, to be ready to act. When the British became aware that the Saudis were moving troops toward Aqaba, perhaps to seize the port, they warned them off. Jordan's armed forces were poorly prepared to deal with the extent of popular unrest.[5]

King Hussein summoned the British ambassador on December 19 to inform him that accession to the Baghdad Pact was impossible; he then dissolved the parliament and called for new elections. The Egyptian media crowed about Hussein's decision. In January Hussein canceled the plan for new elections, and the riots resumed with redoubled violence. This time the king ordered British General Sir John Glubb, the commander of the Jordanian army, or Arab Legion, to put down the unrest with brute force.

In the violence that ensued there were casualties on both sides, including one British officer who was killed in Zarqa on the East Bank.

Our street in the Shaykh Jarrah quarter of Jerusalem witnessed heavy fire by the army as it suppressed the crowds. My family watched the fighting from the comparative safety of the roof, behind high walls. The British army reinforced its strategic reserve in its colony of Cyprus with more paratroopers, and the Royal Air Force base at Mafraq in northern Jordan was reinforced by troops from the RAF Regiment in Iraq.[6] The British feared that if Jordan sank into chaos Israel would take Jerusalem and the West Bank.[7] The Saudis wanted Aqaba and Ma'an.

The unrest was unquestionably abetted by propaganda from Egypt and Saudi Arabia. Nasser was a clear enemy of the pact. The Saudis, too, were opposed to the pact, which they saw as reinforcing their historic rival—the Hashemite family, which ruled in Jordan and Iraq—as well as the British, which were also Saudi enemies. King Saud ibn Abd al Aziz told Hussein that Saudi Arabia was opposed to the expansion of Iraqi influence in the region.[8]

Hussein was at first ambivalent about Nasser. The Egyptian call for Arabs to throw off the colonial yoke resonated with the young man despite his dependence on Britain. His first wife, Dina Abdul Hamid, whom he married in April 1955, was Egyptian born and raised. She came from the Egyptian wing of the Hashemite family, and she was passionately for Nasser. Faisal was the best man at the wedding. So Hussein tried to placate Nasser.[9]

Jordan never joined the Baghdad Pact or its successor organization, the Central Treaty Organization (CENTO). Within a year Hussein sent Glubb back to England, with only one day's notice, to try to shake the image that the king was a puppet of London. In 1956, Nasser emerged as the winner of a crisis over control of the Suez Canal against a conspiracy of Britain, France, and Israel. His popularity was immense across the Arab world, while he had become the bogey man for America in the Middle East.

Nasser, Egypt, and America

It is ironic that Nasser became the villain, because he started out very much as America's man after the July 1952 coup that brought him to power. Nasser was the first native Egyptian to rule his country in the two thousand years since it was conquered by the Roman Empire. His military coup ousted an Albanian monarchy that had been imposed on the country by the Ottoman Empire.

Born January 15, 1918, in Alexandria, Nasser began participating in protests at an early age against the British domination of Egypt. In 1935, he was grazed on the head by a bullet fired by the police to break up a demonstration. He was turned down for admission to the Royal Military Academy in 1937 because of his political activities, but he was admitted on a second application after Nasser used family connections to gain the backing of a senior defense official. He graduated from the academy in 1938 as a second lieutenant. In the academy Nasser made friends with Sadat and other officers who would become the Free Officers movement that toppled King Farouk.[10]

Great Britain controlled Egypt and maintained a large military presence in the country. During World War II the British army defended Egypt from the German and Italian Afrika Korps, which had invaded from Libya. The Egyptian army was sidelined. Sadat was involved in clandestine contacts with the Germans, hoping they would drive the British out of the country.

In May 1948, Egypt joined the Arab coalition fighting Israel. Nasser served in the infantry, and his unit was surrounded by the Israelis at Faluja, north of Gaza, in August 1948 but refused to surrender. Nasser was lightly wounded in the fighting. Only when Israel and Egypt signed an armistice agreement in February 1949 was Faluja occupied by the Israelis, and the 4,000 Egyptian troops, including Nasser, repatriated to Egypt. The siege of Faluja made Nasser a hero in Egypt. Upon their return to Egypt, the country's top singer, Umm Kulthum, gave a concert for the heroes of Faluja.[11] The Palestine war was a watershed for Nasser; according to one of his biographers, it "bolstered his commitment to Arab nationalist principles."[12]

Egypt was ruled by King Farouk, who had ascended to power in 1936. The British forced him to appoint a government favorable to the allies in 1942 after surrounding his palace in Cairo with their tanks. Nonetheless, Egypt was officially neutral in the second world war, until 1945, despite being invaded by Italy and Germany. Farouk was known for his lavish lifestyle, and his regime was corrupt.

The failure of the Egyptian army to save Palestine in 1948 from Israel added to the discontent.

Americans were generally unimpressed by Farouk. When President Franklin Delano Roosevelt visited Egypt in February 1945, his main purpose was to meet the king of Saudi Arabia, Abdul Aziz al Saud, who had impressed FDR greatly. Farouk did not. In the CIA in the early 1950s, Farouk was derisibly nicknamed FF, or "fat fucker."[13]

On July 23, 1952, the Free Officers, a conspiracy of Egyptian military officers, staged a military coup, and Farouk was sent into exile in Monaco and Italy, where he spent the rest of his life. The titular head of the Free Officers was General Muhammad Naguib, but the power rested with Nasser. The Free Officers gave the U.S. embassy in Cairo several hours advance notice of the coup, to help gain American friendship.[14]

The CIA did not help the coup, but it was quick to recognize that the Egyptian revolution was a very important development in the Middle East and one it needed to understand and influence. The CIA's top man in the region was Kermit Roosevelt, a scion of the famous Roosevelt family who was born in Argentina. In February 1952, months before the coup, Roosevelt visited Cairo with the purpose of exploring if "peaceful revolution" was possible under Farouk; that is, could he reform his government? Roosevelt concluded it was not possible. He also held talks with some Free Officers in secret.[15]

After the coup in October 1952, Roosevelt visited Cairo as chief of the CIA's Near East Division, C/NE. When he met with Nasser at the famous Mena House Hotel near the pyramids, each man was "thrilled" with the other, and the CIA began a quiet but not always discreet courtship of the new Egyptian regime.[16]

Nasser was first and foremost an Egyptian nationalist, though he also adopted other leadership roles.[17] His understandable obsession was to break Egypt free of the British and any other foreign power. He was also an Arab nationalist who saw that the mantle of leadership in the Arab world was up for grabs in the 1950s. Until Nasser, Egypt had been a reluctant Arab state; many Egyptians looked down on their fellow Arabs as unsophisticated nomads. Nasser, instead, made Arabism his road to greatness. Nasser also claimed a leadership role in Islam, not in a fundamentalist way, but as another mechanism to establish Egypt's importance and, hence, his own. Finally, Nasser also claimed a leadership role in Africa. He was eager for Egyptian independence to be a harbinger for the independence of the rest of Africa, especially Algeria.

After Dwight David Eisenhower was inaugurated in January 1953, the CIA got new leadership with Allen Dulles, brother of the new secretary of state John Foster Dulles. Both were well-traveled and educated men with years of experience in foreign policy. Allen Dulles had served in the CIA's predecessor organization, the Office of Strategic Services (OSS). During the war he was the OSS chief in Switzerland, where he acquired a reputation for espionage that was probably overrated, but nonetheless widely held.[18] Allen was a man who enjoyed the good life, but he was also smart, pragmatic, and determined to give the president what he wanted. John Foster Dulles was a more ideological man who saw the Cold War with Russia in black-and-white terms, without shades of nuance. He was determined to build an alliance structure extending NATO around the world to contain the Soviet Union and China. Foster Dulles also promised to "roll back" communism, especially in Eastern Europe, which the Soviet Union saw as a threat to control of its allies in the Warsaw Pact.

In May 1953, the secretary of state traveled to Egypt and met publicly with Naguib and, privately, with Nasser. He offered to help quietly arrange an "orderly departure" of British military forces from Egypt, especially from the Suez Canal zone. The British Empire was financially broke after the huge cost of World War II; it had already given up India, the "jewel in the crown" of its empire. Kermit "Kim" Roosevelt Jr., grandson of President Theodore Roosevelt, handled the difficult task of working with London to close its base in Egypt. Prime Minister Winston Churchill was initially against any deal with Cairo, wanting to preserve the British hold on Egypt, but economic factors, especially Britain's huge debts, forced him to accept the closing of the expensive Suez base.[19] A new Anglo-Egyptian Treaty in 1954 sealed the deal.[20] Britain agreed to withdraw its garrison in the Suez Canal zone, 80,000 strong, over the next twenty months. The Suez Canal Company would remain in British hands until 1968.

Miles Copeland was the CIA man in Cairo. At Kim's direction, Copeland often lunched with Nasser, frequently

16

in Nasser's office. Allen Dulles wanted "to harness Arab nationalism" for American purposes, to align the United States with the forces of anti-colonialism that were sweeping Africa and Asia.[21] The agency helped the new regime set up its intelligence service and its propaganda apparatus.[22]

Nasser's allure was boosted enormously on October 24, 1954, when, as he was speaking in Alexandria to a large audience, eight shots rang out. Nasser paused only for an instant and then continued his speech, more eloquent and passionate than ever. The would-be assassin was a member of the Muslim Brotherhood.

Israel watched nervously as Nasser gained power and influence, especially leery of his ties to Washington. The Israeli Secret Intelligence Service, Mossad, tried to disrupt those ties with a poorly conceived covert operation. Egyptian Jews were recruited to put bombs in the American libraries in Cairo and Alexandria. Others targeted cinemas and post offices. Operation Suzannah was quickly uncovered by the Egyptians, and two of the bombers were executed.[23]

The United States, United Kingdom, and France imposed an arms embargo on Israel and the Arab states in 1950 to discourage an arms race. The Tripartite Declaration was initially successful in calming tensions. In February 1955, the Baghdad Pact was signed in Iraq, which seemed to open a door for Iran, Turkey, Pakistan, and Iraq to get access to Western arms. Nasser, as noted earlier, denounced the pact. Just days later Israel carried out a major cross-border raid into Egyptian-occupied Gaza in

17

response to terrorist attacks staged out of Gaza. On February 28, 1955, the Operation Black Arrow raid killed thirty-six Egyptian and Palestinian soldiers. It was a major turning point in the Arab-Israeli conflict. Nasser was determined to get arms.[24]

In 1955, the CIA gave Nasser $3 million to use for purchasing arms. Nasser saw the offer as insignificant and more bribe than help. He secured a much better arms deal, worth $250 million, with Czechoslovakia, a Soviet puppet state. The arms included 150 MiG-15 jet fighters and 230 T-34 tanks, blowing a hole in the tripartite arms embargo. The CIA team in Cairo tried to portray the deal as an understandable reaction to the Gaza raid and even persuaded Nasser to emphasize that the weapons were Czech, not Soviet. John Foster Dulles did not buy it, and he turned against Nasser.[25]

Ironically, Nasser used the CIA money to build a tower in Cairo for his Voice of the Arabs radio station. The tower became famous in Egypt, variously called "Roosevelt's Foundation" or "Roosevelt's Erection."[26] The Czech arms deal signaled the end of the CIA honeymoon with Nasser, although on March 26, 1956, Eisenhower awarded Kim Roosevelt the National Security Medal in a secret ceremony in the White House for his role in Egypt and his more famous role in the 1953 coup in Iran that firmly installed the Shah in power.[27]

Relations between Egypt and the Western powers quickly deteriorated after 1955. The Czech arms deal was one reason. Egypt was also supporting the Algerian struggle for independence from France and pushing for more control over the Suez Canal from Britain. Nasser supported the Palestinians against Israel, and attacks into Israel accelerated from both Gaza and Jordan's West Bank.

The 1956 Suez Crisis

Nasser was unwittingly pushing his enemies into a conspiracy against him. The first cabal was between France and Israel. Egypt's support for the Algerian independence war persuaded Paris to begin selling arms to Israel even before the Czech deal; after the deal, Israel was desperate for weapons and France was eager to help. A major arms deal was signed in April 1956.

Events in Jordan pushed Great Britain into the emerging conspiracy against Egypt. Shaken by the Baghdad Pact riots, King Hussein dismissed Sir John Bagot Glubb, known as Glubb Pasha, from command of the Jordanian military on March 1, 1956. Glubb had loyally served both the British and Jordanian crowns since the 1920s as a soldier in the British-run Arab Legion in Jordan. In 1939, he became the commander of the Arab Legion and made it the best military formation in the Arab world; it helped London control much of the Middle East in World War II. In 1948, Glubb led the Jordanian Royal Army, as it was now called, in the war against Israel, and he succeeded in acquiring the West Bank and East Jerusalem for Jordan.

Glubb Pasha had also quelled the Baghdad Pact riots. But King Hussein increasingly resented the role played by the much older general in the Kingdom. Moreover, Hussein realized that British control of the army only reinforced the Arab nationalism that fed the riots. Britain controlled Jordan through Glubb Pasha. The king gave the general only one day to collect his family and his possessions, and expelled him and many other British officers from Jordan permanently, replacing them with Jordanian officers. Among those sent back to London was Colonel Patrick Coghill, the chief of intelligence for Jordan. The king effectively took over his job.[28] Glubb Pasha never returned to Jordan, but the king would later deliver the eulogy at his funeral in Westminster Abbey in April 1986, praising his service to "his second country, Jordan, at a crucial moment in its history and development."[29]

In London, Prime Minister Anthony Eden was furious. He blamed Nasser for the ousting of Glubb Pasha. It was true that the Voice of the Arabs had called for the removal of British officers from command of the Jordanian army, but that was Hussein's decision, not Nasser's. Hussein assured the British that he was still a friend (he needed their financial subsidies). Eden was convinced it was Nasser who had ended Britain's domination of Jordan—just as it had ended London's control of Egypt—and he began to seek Nasser's demise. It became an obsession for him.

The 1956 Suez Crisis has been well covered in several excellent histories. It was a crucial turning point in modern Middle Eastern politics and in the decline of the European colonial empires. It is also a fascinating study in conspiracy. Three close American allies—Israel, France, and the United Kingdom—secretly plotted to attack Egypt. They were especially determined to keep the secret of their conspiracy from the United States and, especially, the American president. Eisenhower, the liberator of France who had led the Anglo-American invasion of D-Day, was to be kept in the dark.

It was Jordan and its conflict with Israel that most hampered the development of the tripartite conspiracy against Nasser. Throughout much of 1956, firefights along the cease-fire line between Jordan and Israel threatened to provoke a broader conflict. Terrorist attacks by Palestinians inside Israel led to Israeli retaliation, often with high Jordanian casualties. The conflict seemed to be escalating all summer and into the fall.

Great Britain had a defense treaty with Jordan. Even after the departure of Glubb Pasha, Prime Minister Eden and his cabinet felt obligated to defend Jordan from attack. London was convinced the Israelis wanted an opportunity to seize the West Bank and East Jerusalem from Jordan, leaving the Hashemite Kingdom much reduced. British military planners developed a contingency plan to come to Jordan's assistance to stop the Israelis. Operation Cordage was being contemplated even as the British began planning Operation Musketeer, the code name for the invasion of Egypt.

In May 1956, Nasser officially recognized the communist People's Republic of China as the legitimate government of China. The Eisenhower administration was dedicated to supporting the nationalist government in

Formosa as the legitimate Chinese government with a seat at the United Nations Security Council. In response to the Egyptian move, Eisenhower withdrew an offer for American financial aid to Egypt to build a dam on the Nile River at Aswan. The dam project was the centerpiece of Nasser's plan to improve the living standards of the Egyptian people.

In a dramatic response on July 26, 1956, in a speech to 100,000 Egyptians in Liberation Square in Alexandria, Nasser announced the nationalization of the Suez Canal. Egyptian troops took control of the canal, and all the assets of the British Suez Canal Company were seized. Nasser also announced that the canal would be closed to Israeli shipping and that Egypt would also close the Straits of Tiran to shipping bound for the Israeli port at Eilat.

Nasser had deftly struck at what London believed was the jugular vein of the British Empire. For almost a century the canal had been the lifeline of the empire, from London to India and beyond. A third of the ships that transited the canal each year were British, and the British government held a 44 percent stake in the Suez Canal Company, making it the largest stockholder (France was second). Seventy percent of Western Europe's oil passed through the canal from the Persian Gulf.[30] Nasser now controlled Europe's oil.

Prime Minister Eden was hosting a dinner in London for Iraq's King Faisal II and his prime minister Nuri al Said when the news of Nasser's announcement arrived. The Iraqis urged Eden to strike back; they wanted their nemesis destroyed by the British. Eden denounced the nationalization of the canal as aggression and labeled Nasser a new Hitler. The French and Israelis agreed secretly to take military action against Egypt in late July.

For the next three months, the United States tried to devise a diplomatic solution to the crisis around the canal, but to no avail. Meanwhile the French and Israelis secretly began devising a plan to attack Egypt. The British were reluctant to work with Israel, preferring an Anglo-French operation without the Israelis. Concern about the future of Jordan was the principal British concern. But by October 1956, Eden was won over by the French to a tripartite operation that would be kept secret from Washington.

The plan would begin with an Israeli attack on Egypt in the Gaza Strip and the Sinai Peninsula. Israel would open the Straits of Tiran by seizing all of the Sinai. As Israeli troops approached the canal, the British and French would intervene and seize the canal, allegedly to protect it from the war between Egypt and Israel but, in fact, to take it from Nasser. The plan was based on the assumption that Nasser would fall from office if the canal was seized, a dubious assumption at best.

What the Americans knew about the plot is a matter of much historical investigation. Recent scholarship suggests that the CIA had some warning of the plot. The American Defense Attaché in Tel Aviv reported the massive mobilization of the Israel Defense Forces (IDF) on October 26. Director of the CIA Allen Dulles learned of the tripartite plot sometime in late October from a French source, and CIA

U2 aircraft monitored the British and French navies, load-
ing men and supplies in Marseilles, Malta, and Cyprus. At
the same time, James Jesus Angleton, the head of coun-
terintelligence in the agency as well as chief of the Israel
desk, told Allen that his Israeli counterparts denied any
attack was coming.[31]

Eisenhower reacted to the tripartite attack harshly, no
doubt angered by a sense of betrayal by his allies. His reelection was imminent, and another crisis was underway
in Eastern Europe, where Russia was facing an uprising
in Hungary against its puppet government. Eisenhower
believed the Anglo-French-Israeli plot undermined any
effort to stop Russia from restoring its control of Hungary.
Certainly it weakened the moral position of the West as the
defender of liberty.

At the end of October 1956, the Israelis launched their
attack on Sinai, Operation Kadesh, and they quickly prevailed over the Egyptians. The Israel Defense Forces over-
ran Gaza, seized Sharm al Shaykh, and advanced on the
canal. In early November, the British and French began
their military operations around Port Said, the northern terminus of the canal. The United States advanced a
resolution in the Security Council demanding an immediate cease-fire and the withdrawal of the Israelis from
Egyptian territory. The British and French vetoed it. On
November 2, 1956, the United Nations General Assembly
voted 65 to 5 to demand a cease-fire; full withdrawal of all
Israeli, French, and British forces; and the reopening of
the canal, which had been closed due to the fighting. Only

Australia and New Zealand joined the tripartite plotters in voting no.

The closure of the canal resulted in oil tankers going around Africa to carry oil from the Persian Gulf to Europe. The Syrian government shut down the Trans-Arabia pipeline that brought Iraqi oil to the Mediterranean. Oil prices spiked in Europe, putting economic pressure on Paris and London. King Saud of Saudi Arabia then announced a total embargo on oil sales to France and England.

Eisenhower spoke to the nation virtually on the eve of the November election and called for full withdrawal by the three American allies from Egypt. He also applied financial pressure behind the scenes. British Chancellor of the Exchequer Harold Macmillan told Prime Minister Eden the British economy was on the verge of disaster, and on November 6 the United Kingdom accepted a cease-fire without consulting its two partners. France and Israel followed soon after. Eden resigned in January 1957 and was succeeded by Macmillan, a longtime Eisenhower friend and colleague.

Macmillan recognized the urgent need to mend fences with his old friend, but he was just as hard on Nasser as Eden had been. He had labeled Nasser "an Asiatic Mussolini." Macmillan believed that if Nasser won the Suez Crisis, it would mean, according to historian William Hitchcock, "the destruction of Great Britain as a first-class power and its reduction to a status similar to that of Holland." But Eisenhower, Hitchcock adds, believed Nasser had positioned himself as the embodiment of independence and had the Muslim world "from Dakar to the Philippines against us."[32]

The United Nations, at Canada's initiative, created a peacekeeping force to replace the British and French troops in the canal, which was reopened. The Secretary-General of the United Nations, Dag Hammarskjold, put together the force and equipped the troops with distinctive blue helmets to underscore their neutrality. Then the United Nations Emergency Force (UNEF) was used to monitor the Israeli-Egyptian armistice line. It took months and significant American pressure before the Israelis finally, and grudgingly, completed a full withdrawal from the Sinai and Gaza.

During the Suez Crisis, the Soviet Union crushed the uprising in Budapest. The Eisenhower administration was unable to do anything to assist the Hungarian revolution against communism, and John Foster Dulles' promises that the United States would roll back communism in Europe were exposed as empty rhetoric. Eisenhower believed the tripartite attack on Egypt had materially aided the Soviets in Hungary by diverting attention, especially in Asia and Africa, from the Russians' brutality.

The Soviets also intervened in the Suez Crisis directly. Soviet Premier Nikolai Bulganin sent letters to his counterparts in London, Paris, and Tel Aviv, threatening rocket attacks on their cities if they did not withdraw their forces from Egypt. The letter to Israeli Prime Minister David Ben Gurion warned that "Israel is playing with the fate of peace . . . which will place a question upon the very existence of Israel as a State."[33] The threats quickly became public, and Moscow would take credit for the cease-fire and withdrawal as the result of its rocket rattling.

At the time, Washington did not know if the Russian threats were real or bluffs. The American intelligence community had insufficient information on the status of Russia's ballistic missile capability, and Eisenhower had to worry that the threats were real. We know now that they were not; Moscow was bluffing. But in the late 1950s, Moscow looked to be winning the missile race and the space race. Just a year after the canal crisis, in October 1957, the Soviets launched the first ever satellite into orbit, Sputnik.

Nasser was the big winner from the 1956 crisis. For the first time in centuries an Egyptian leader had stood up to the imperial powers of Europe and emerged victorious. Nasser had evicted the British from Egypt, taken control of the Suez Canal, and humiliated a British prime minister into resignation. Nasser had rebuffed the French, as well, dealing them a defeat that would help inspire the Algerian people to continue their war for freedom. Nasser had also thwarted Israel's attempt to seize and keep the Sinai Peninsula and the Gaza Strip. UNEF seemed a small price to pay for victory. Nasser could also point to his *entente* with Russia as having played a role in his victory. Of course, the United States had been crucial to his success, but Nasser did not give Eisenhower any credit, at least in public.

Nasser was not only the undisputed leader of Egypt, he was the charismatic leader of the Arab peoples, from

Morocco to Oman. At least that was the image he sought to portray. Moreover, he had emerged as one of the key leaders of the newly independent states of Asia and Africa, along with India's Nehru and Indonesia's Sukarno. No Egyptian had played such a role on the world stage since Cleopatra.

The Eisenhower Doctrine

President Eisenhower was probably the greatest American hero of the twentieth century. He was also the last great general elected to the White House. Before Ike, his nickname, generals were a common feature of presidential politics, from George Washington to Zachary Taylor and Ulysses Grant. Since Ike, no general has successfully run for the Oval Office.

Ike's hero status was well earned. After studying at West Point, Eisenhower served with distinction in the U.S. Army. He was commander of the allied forces that invaded North Africa in 1942, when he first began to work with Macmillan. In June 1944, he was commander of the allied invasion of France, D-Day, the largest amphibious operation in history. He commanded the 3 million-man-strong allied armies advancing across France and the low countries into Germany. As his memoir described it, this was a crusade in Europe and he was the leader of the allied forces that defeated Nazi Germany. After the war, he was commander of the NATO military command in Europe. In short, he was a consummate leader of allies embodying the idea that America is strong because it has strong alliances.

He was also a religious man. Ike is the only American president ever to have been baptized while in office; in fact, just a few days after his inauguration. He also began National Security Council (NSC) meetings with a prayer. He was close to the great religious leaders of America of his time, such as men like Billy Graham.[34] Ike's religious faith helped underscore his interest in supporting American allies in the Middle East who shared his aversion to atheism.

Eisenhower also understood that the days of imperialism were over. America needed to reach out to the Third World, a phrase that had been coined in 1952 to describe the newly emerging nations in Asia and Africa. In December 1956, Ike invited the leader of India, Prime Minister Jawaharlal Nehru, to Washington for three full days of discussion. In an unprecedented gesture of welcome, Ike hosted Nehru for an overnight visit in his home in Gettysburg, Pennsylvania, where Nehru gave his account of how the Suez and Budapest crises had played out in the Third World.[35]

By the beginning of 1957, it was apparent to the president that America's relationships with its key allies were in considerable disrepair. The Suez Crisis, especially the deliberate decision of three close allies to conceal their plans from Washington, had gravely damaged the West's position in the Middle East. Most important, the special relationship with the United Kingdom was in trouble.

Crucial to the new strategy was to find Arab alterna-
tives to Nasser; that is, Arab allies that could confront
Egypt. This was a daunting task after Suez. Saudi Arabia
was America's preference, given the longstanding close
ties in the oil industry and Franklin Roosevelt's successful
meeting with King Saud in February 1945. But the Kingdom was militarily weak, the economy suffered from King
Saud's mismanagement, and the country was sparsely
populated. Iraq was a stronger alternative to Egypt, with a
larger army, more advanced economy, and a larger population. But the Saudi-Hashemite divide was still intense,
so Washington would need to work with both Arab monarchies and the British to try to fashion a new alternative
to Nasser.[36]

Eisenhower responded with a speech to Congress in
January 1957 in which he laid out what would be called
the Eisenhower Doctrine for the Middle East. He did not
revisit the quarrels of 1956; the speech did not assign
blame for the events of 1956 or seek to humiliate any U.S.
allies. Nor was it a diatribe against Nasser.

Instead, Eisenhower tried to explain in his speech why
the Middle East mattered to Americans and the threat
that was posed by the Soviet Union and communism to the
region. He laid out a strategy for defending Western interests in the region, the most detailed and specific explanation for American intervention in the Middle East any
president had ever provided. It would also form the basis
for the Marines' intervention in Beirut in July 1958.

On January 5, 1957, Eisenhower told Congress that

"the Middle East has abruptly reached a new and critical stage in its long and important history."[37] The Suez Crisis had brought the region to a new level of instability, which, Eisenhower explained, "at times is manipulated by International Communism."[38] The president noted that "Russia's rulers have long sought to dominate the Middle East."[39]

Eisenhower laid out in his speech to the Congress America's key interests in the region. First and foremost was oil. Two-thirds of the "presently known oil deposits of the world" were in the Middle East, he noted, which was crucial to the economies of the world's nations, but especially to Europe. If a hostile power controlled the region's oil, the "free nations would be placed in serious jeopardy." Second were "other factors which transcend the material" because the region is the birthplace of "three great religions—Moslem, Christian, and Hebrew. Mecca and Jerusalem are more than places on a map. They symbolize religions which teach that the spirit has supremacy over matter." The three great religions affirm that the "individual has a dignity and rights of which no despotic government can rightfully deprive him." The president said it would be "intolerable if the holy places of the Middle East should be subjected to a rule that glorifies atheistic matters." Eisenhower did not place the survival of Israel itself as a vital American security interest.

To prevent Soviet domination of the Middle East, Eisenhower asked Congress to give him the authority to "cooperate with and assist any nation or group of nations" to maintain their independence, including by the "employment of the armed forces of the United States to secure and protect the territorial integrity and independence of such nations" if they request American help against "overt armed aggression from any nation controlled by International Communism." He thought Congress should also authorize economic and military assistance programs to threatened nations in the region who requested aid.

The speech emphasized the "authority to employ the armed forces" of the United States in the Middle East. It was the first time a president had identified the region as a vital American interest that needed to be defended by American combat troops. The Eisenhower Doctrine is a crucial milestone in America's engagement in the Middle East. The president understood he was expanding America's global footprint and taking on a role that "involves certain burdens and indeed risks for the United States."

Congress voted to support the president. The House of Representatives endorsed the doctrine in late January by a vote of 355 to 61 and the Senate on March 5, 1957, 72 to 18. Eisenhower had broken new ground. The United States was now on record committed to the defense of the Middle East. As William Hitchcock, his preeminent biographer, later wrote, "in January 1957 Eisenhower declared that the United States would fight to protect its interests in the Middle East; more than six decades later it is fighting still."[40]

Two

DAMASCUS AND RIYADH

Policymakers often turn to their security and intelligence services when they want a fairly quick and cheap solution to a complex and difficult political challenge abroad. My experience in thirty years in the government, including working for four presidents in the White House directly, underscores the allure of covert action for chief executives. In 1953, President Dwight David Eisenhower turned to the CIA to rid himself of a nationalist government in Iran. Kermit Roosevelt, the agency's master spy, produced Operation Ajax, which ousted the nationalists in a military coup and restored the Shah to power. The Iran coup gave CIA director Allen Dulles new standing in Eisenhower's eyes and made Kermit Roosevelt famous (decades later, he would write a book about the affair).[1]

Five years later, America's oldest ally in the Arab world, Saudi Arabia, tried to emulate Roosevelt and rid itself of the danger posed by Arab nationalists and revolutionaries by sponsoring a coup in Syria. King Saud, who had ascended to the throne in 1953 when his father Abd Al Aziz al Saud, the founder of the modern Kingdom, died, was Eisenhower's personal choice to be the American antithesis to Gamal Abd al Nasser. The king would rally the Arabs to America's side in the Cold War. Washington knew the Saudis were working on a coup in Damascus; the Saudis had told them so.

Unfortunately for Saud, the coup was a half-baked scheme, more like a provocation and a set-up. The Egyptians and Syrians, now united in the United Arab Republic, were aware of the conspiracy and announced it to the world on March 5, 1958. Saud would be the major victim of the coup he had plotted. On March 24, the Saudi royal family convened in Riyadh and transferred most of Saud's powers to his brother, Crown Prince Faisal. Ike's alternative to Nasser was still king but was now without the power to rule. The failed coup also inaugurated the crisis that would lead to the Marine landing in Beirut.

Damascus

Syria is an old country with new, artificial borders. For most of history, the name *Syria* referred to the region that now includes the nations of Syria, Lebanon, Israel, Jordan, and the Palestinian territories. The current bor-

*President Dwight David Eisenhower, King
Saud, and Vice President Richard Nixon.*

ders of Syria were drawn a century ago, at the end of the
First World War. The Ottoman Empire picked the wrong
side of the war, lost, and was dissolved after centuries of
dominating the Arab world while the winners of the war,
France and the United Kingdom, carved up the Ottoman's
lands. France got Syria and Lebanon; the United Kingdom
took Iraq and Palestine, which then included Jordan. The
French and British drew the borders. The rump state of
Syria lost most of its coastline on the Mediterranean Sea.
The Arabs tried to resist, but the French army was too
powerful.

After the French were defeated by Nazi Germany in
1940, British forces, including the Arab Legion, took con-

trol of Syria and Lebanon by force. At the end of the war, the winners, led by the United States, pushed France to give Lebanon and Syria their independence. In 1919, Lebanon probably had a majority Christian population, but a large Muslim minority. In Lebanon, the French had imposed a national charter on the small country's politics: the pro-French Maronite Christian community would always provide the nation's president; the Sunni Muslim community would provide the prime minister; and the Shia Muslims would provide the speaker of the parliament. This formula would keep Lebanon within the French sphere of influence, in theory.

Syria was even more complicated. Arab Sunni Muslims are the majority of the population, but there are sizable minorities of Arab Christians, Druze, Kurds, and Alawites, a distinct religious community that considers itself Muslim. A weak republic was created by the French as they left in 1946, and it was doomed to failure.

Syrians felt a pervasive loss of identity. According to journalist Patrick Seale, the new state's borders seemed, to many, to be foreign-imposed butchery or "amputation" of their country.[2] Lebanon and Palestine were integral parts of Syria that had been torn away by European colonialism. The creation of Israel added to the identity challenge. The Zionist movement to create a Jewish state in what had historically been southern Syria, with its capital in al Quds al Arabi—Jerusalem—was a direct challenge to most Syrians' sense of identity.

Defeat in 1948 by the Israelis after a lackluster military

performance by the Syrian army created by the French only made things worse. Syrians felt ashamed of their army's failure, and officers in the army were particularly outraged, blaming the civilian government for the defeat.

For the next twenty years, Syria was the playground of every foreign intelligence service in the Middle East, each backing different military cabals and political parties to control Syria. Coup followed coup in a dizzying pattern. One of the most important political parties was the Ba'ath, or Renaissance, Party, which stood for the unification of all Arabs into a new political state, from Morocco to Oman, a return to the greatness of the Arab empires of the eighth and ninth centuries, especially the Umayyads, which had ruled all the Islamic world from their capital in Damascus. A small but important Communist Party was also active in the intrigues in Syria in the 1950s.

The first coup came in March 1949. The Syrian government had turned to Russia, after its defeat by Israel, for arms, and Czechoslovakia was used as the cut-out for the arms deal, a situation that greatly alarmed Washington. In addition to its war with Israel, Syria was also demanding the return of the province of Alexandretta, historically part of Syria but awarded to Turkey by France on the eve of World War II to encourage Turkey not to join with Germany and Italy in the approaching global conflict. Turkey appealed to Washington for support. There were also disputes with the major oil companies, who wanted to build a trans-Arabia pipeline from the Persian Gulf to the Mediterranean coast of Syria.

Beginning in November 1948, the CIA began court-
ing disgruntled Syrian army officers. Army Chief of
Staff Husni Zaim was the main plotter. Virulently anti-
communist and anti-Soviet, Zaim was not a particularly
bright individual. According to Douglas Little, his CIA
handlers reported to Washington that "he did not have the
competence of a French corporal," but he was strongly opposed to Russia.[3] On March 30, 1949, Zaim seized power
and arrested the elected president. He then promptly arrested dozens of communists.

Zaim came from the minority Druze Muslim community, which is centered in southern Syria near Jordan.
Historically, the Druze have been a closed society and are
regarded as heretics by many Sunni Muslims. The French
had deliberately chosen Druze candidates for the officer
corps because they were more likely to stay loyal to Paris
(they also discriminated in favor of Alawites, another
small Muslim sect).

Zaim reached out to the United States after seizing
power and offered to start negotiations for a peace treaty
with Israel and to resettle 250,000 Palestinian refugees in
Syria; he also banned the Communist Party. In July 1949,
he withdrew all Syrian claims to Alexandretta and signed
an armistice agreement with Israel. The trans-Arabia oil
pipeline deal was set.

Zaim's dealings with Israel did him in. His opening to
Israel was regarded as a betrayal of Syrian identity by most
of the army, and on August 14, 1949, he was overthrown
in another coup and executed. The new government an-

nounced plans to merge Syria with Iraq's Hashemite dynasty. Another coup, the third in less than a year, followed on December 19, 1949, by army officers opposed to a merger with Iraq.

The December coup was led by Colonel Adib Shishakli, who was also anti-communist, but cleverer than Zaim. American officials were aware of his plans to seize power and welcomed his coup. When Eisenhower became president, Secretary of State John Foster Dulles visited Damascus in May 1953 and was impressed by Shishakli. Dulles told Eisenhower "Syria was a state that offered real possibilities" for the United States.[4]

Another coup came in February 1954, however, and brought into power army officers with close connections to the Ba'ath and Communist parties. The Communist Party boss, Khalid Bakdash, was elected to the Syrian parliament, and the country tilted aggressively toward Moscow. John Foster Dulles characterized Syria now as "a Soviet satellite." His brother, CIA chief Allen Dulles, said "the situation in Syria is the worst of all countries in the area."[5] Soviet arms began arriving in large quantities into Syria.

Washington and London conspired to oust the new regime in Damascus. The plot was called Operation Straggle and was tentatively timed for late October 1956. Allen Dulles and Kermit Roosevelt traveled to London in March 1956 to work on the details of the plot. Planning for Straggle continued through the summer and fall, but the British, at the last minute, pushed back the date for the coup by four days, without telling the CIA they were doing so, so the coup would coincide with the Israeli invasion of Sinai and the Suez Crisis. A coup in Damascus would add to the pressure on Nasser.[6]

It was a plot too far. Syrian intelligence discovered the Straggle plotters and arrested them. The Syrian president flew to Moscow and supported Russia's threats to bomb London, Paris, and Tel Aviv. Nasser appeared on the Syrian political scene, and Syrians found a new hero, a Saladin to reunite Arabia, restore Arab dignity, and wipe away the shame of the French borders and the creation of Israel. Nasser's victory over the British-French-Israeli conspiracy in 1956 added luster to the Syrians for Nasser. His enemies, especially Iraq's Hashemites, fought back and tried to find allies among Syria's privileged elites, who feared revolution would undermine their position.

In July 1957, Syria signed a $500 million grain-for-weapons arms deal with Russia. In the next month, Syria expelled three CIA officers from the country for plotting another coup, and the U.S. embassy was put under around-the-clock surveillance. Eisenhower expelled the Syrian ambassador from Washington in retaliation. The Syrians then expelled the American ambassador from Damascus. In his memoirs, Eisenhower relates that he considered encouraging Turkey and Iraq to invade Syria, but upon reflection, he decided against such a draconian move. It took several months to persuade the Turks, who had mobilized on the Syrian border, to back down.[7]

King Saud helped resolve the crisis by traveling to Beirut and Damascus in September 1957 and by claiming

Syria was not a threat to Turkey while, at the same time, promising Saudi support for Syrian sovereignty. Briefly, Saud appeared to be the leader of the Arab world.

Then Nasser outflanked him. Syrian military officers, led by Colonel Abdul Hamid Sarraj, the head of Syrian intelligence (the Deuxième Bureau), secretly traveled to Cairo to appeal for Egyptian help. In his book *The Struggle for Syria*, Patrick Seale describes how on October 13, 1957, several thousand Egyptian troops landed in Latakia, Syria, to "take up battle positions in northern Syria side by side with their Syrian brothers." Saudi Arabia had promised to defend Syria; Egypt had acted to defend Syria. "Speech making by politicians lagged far behind the example of close" military cooperation, Seale notes.[8] Nasser, not Saud, emerged as the hero of the crisis.

On February 1, 1958, the United Arab Republic was created. Syria unified itself with Nasser, though it was not his idea. In fact, when the Syrians first approached him in January, Nasser initially resisted the proposal to unite the two countries because they were separated by Israel. He realized that the physical separation was a major barrier to real unity. But the weak government in Damascus, which was a coalition of several groups, including Ba'athists, was determined that their survival was only possible if they aligned with Nasser and if Syria went out of existence. The Ba'ath were especially worried by the strength of the Syrian Communist Party, led by Bakdash, which they feared would launch a coup and take power. It is an irony that the United Arab Republic (UAR) was created in part by fear of communism, since Washington would come to portray the UAR as a veritable arm of international communism.

Nasser drove a hard bargain. He insisted that a merger must come along with the dissolution of all political parties in Syria, including both the Ba'ath and the communists as well as any other. The Syrian officer corps must quit playing politics. He would become president with a new parliament and a new constitution. The Egyptian flag—the Arab nationalist banner with horizontal bars of red, white, and black—would become the UAR flag, but with two stars: one for Egypt and one for Syria. The Syrian politicians who had come to Cairo to ask for unity had no choice now but to accept Nasser's terms. He would move to oust many of them from power, arrest the communist leadership, and put Egyptians in charge of most of Syrian decisionmaking.

The news of the merger on February 1 was met with massive crowds of Syrians chanting Nasser's name, much like I had heard in Jerusalem three years before. Crowds poured through Cairo and Alexandria at the news, as well, enchanted that an Egyptian was leading the Arab world. Nasser flew to Damascus, which he had never before visited, and was driven directly to the tomb of Salah al Din al Ayyubi, the Islamic warrior who had defeated the Crusaders in 1187, in a powerful symbolic act.

Elsewhere in the region, there was fear and trepidation. The monarchs of the Arab world were the most fearful. One of their number, Farouk, had already fallen to

Nasser. Who was next? How could the tide of revolution be stopped from sweeping every king away? Were the Arab world's monarchs going to tumble away like a line of dominoes?

The Hashemites were the first to react. On February 14, 1958, King Faisal in Iraq and King Hussein in Jordan announced an Arab Federation that would bring their two countries together in a confederation under Faisal. Baghdad would be the capital. King Hussein would continue to rule in Jordan, but in a secondary position to his cousin in Iraq. The bureaucracies and armies of the two states would eventually be merged, but the timeframe for that was kept open. The Arab world was split in two, with Nasser's UAR facing the Hashemites Federation.

Riyadh

The House of Saud was just as worried as its old nemesis, the House of Hashim. King Saud had good reason to be worried. He and his country were financially broke because he had spent the Kingdom's oil wealth on his own entertainment and corruption. He was a notorious gambler and drank far too much Cointreau. Much of the royal family had become disillusioned about Saud, and that disillusionment had turned to active campaigning to limit his powers or even depose him. There was no precedent for doing so, however, in the history of the Saudi kingdoms going back to 1744. When the royal family became divided, as happened often in the late 1800s, it fell into civil war. No one in the family wanted that, but pressure to clip Saud's power was building.

For Eisenhower and the Dulles brothers, however, Saud was their man. They hoped Saud could become the answer to Nasser, a pro-West charismatic figure who could galvanize Arab nationalism behind a man solidly in the American camp. Saudi Arabia was America's oldest ally in the Arab world, the American oil companies were dominant in the Kingdom, and the U.S. Air Force had a base in Dhahran that had its origins in World War II. "The King could be built up, possibly as a spiritual leader first," Ike told his aides, using his status as the defender of the two holy mosques in Mecca and Medina.[9]

Moreover, the Saudis were cool to the United Kingdom. There were outstanding border disputes between the Saudis and the British protectorates that hugged the coast of the Persian Gulf, particularly over the Buraimi Oasis, which was claimed both by Saudi Arabia and what was then called the Trucial States (today the United Arab Emirates). The Saudis were also the longstanding opponents of the Hashemites, which Britain had put in power in Jordan and Iraq. Washington felt the Saudis were a more comfortable ally than the Hashemites and that Saud was a more likely leader of Arab nationalists friendly to America than the Hashemites, who were widely seen as British puppets. The Saudis broke relations with the United Kingdom during the Suez Crisis and cut off oil.

King Saud visited Washington in late January and early February 1957. He was the first Saudi king to visit the United States. Eisenhower met the king upon his arrival at National Airport, an unprecedented sign of the importance of the visit and the visitor.[10] The royal party exceeded eighty people, including some of Saud's wives and children. They were so numerous that Blair House, the official guest house of the White House, could not manage the entire party, and some of Saud's bodyguards pitched tents on Lafayette Square. What had been planned as a three-day visit stretched to nine days. The king met with Ike and Vice President Nixon, as well as many cabinet members and members of Congress. There were numerous official dinners and lunches.

Iraq's Crown Prince Abdallah was also in Washington, and he and Saud met. That meeting reinforced Saud's credentials to Ike and led to a brief reduction in tension between Saudi Arabia and Iraq.[11]

King Saud held a dinner in honor of Eisenhower. As American diplomat Patrick Hart observed, "the scene was lavish in the extreme, with a huge guest list and an ice sculpture as the centerpiece of the extended banquet hall." The whole performance was to build up Saud as the counterweight to Nasser, "an idea that proved to be a miscalculation," according to Hart.[12]

The official communique at the end of the visit noted that "Saudi Arabia, by virtue of its spiritual, geographical and economic position, is of vital importance" to the Middle East and world peace. While Saud did not directly endorse the Eisenhower Doctrine, he expressed support for its objectives and appreciation for the president's "exposition" of its purpose. The two countries agreed to extend the lease for the Dhahran Airfield for an additional five years. The United States would also provide training for the Royal Guards, two regular divisions of the Saudi Army, as well as tanks and aircraft.[13]

Throughout 1957, Ike regarded Saud as his alternative to Nasser. American diplomacy sought to portray the Saudi king as the true leader of the Arab and Islamic worlds, one that was pro-American and an enthusiastic opponent of international communism. The Saudis had no relations with Russia, and the Americans had quietly supported Saud's efforts to resolve the Syria-Turkey crisis in the fall of 1957.

On March 3, 1958, King Saud met with the American ambassador in Saudi Arabia. At the end of the meeting, the Keeper of the Privy Purse, Saud's closest aide, took the ambassador aside for a moment. He told the ambassador that the king wanted Eisenhower to know that "a successful military revolution would take place within a few days in Syria." The king wanted this information conveyed to the president and Secretary Dulles in the shortest possible time, and he hoped for a response.[14]

Eisenhower responded immediately to the king's message about an impending coup in Damascus by saying that he appreciated the confidence the king was demonstrating in Washington on a crucial issue. It was a positive response. Behind the scenes, the American embassy in Damascus expressed "serious doubts" about the "bona fides" of the Saudi-backed plot. The American ambassador in Syria told Washington that he feared the plot was a provocation to discredit Saud.[15] The CIA also told Eisenhower that Saud's plot was probably compromised and that Saud "was falling into a trap," as Eisenhower later wrote in his memoirs.[16]

It was too late. On March 5, 1958, Nasser announced in a speech in Damascus that King Saud was behind a plot to assassinate him and break up the UAR by a coup in Syria. Nasser's head of Syrian intelligence, Abdul Hamid Sarraj, confessed that the Saudis had given him 2 million British pounds to put a bomb on board Nasser's plane to blow up the Egyptian leader. The Egyptian government gave to the press three checks from the Saudis to the Syrian plotters to prove their case. Nasser labeled Saud an enemy of the Arab people and a puppet of the West.[17] The Egyptian propaganda machine took off after the king.

The next day, CIA director Allen Dulles told the National Security Council (NSC) that "a dramatic development had occurred over the course of last night. Nasser was now fully engaged in an all-out battle with the remaining pro-Western Arab leaders." More specifically, Dulles warned that "King Saud's position is gravely endangered by these developments." Dulles told Eisenhower that the king's position was so weakened by the exposure of the Syrian plot that it constituted a trend that could lead to the collapse of the pro-Western regimes in Iraq, Jordan, and elsewhere in the Near East, "and we may find that the USSR will take over control of this whole oil-rich area." The director concluded: "the situation is extremely grave."[18]

In an urgent message to Riyadh, Eisenhower expressed his strong support for Saud in the face of the "attacks by UAR against His Majesty" on the Voice of the Arabs. The State Department, like the CIA, "had grave apprehensions concerning the possible results for Saud."[19]

It was an extraordinarily bleak assessment that would have repercussions for the rest of 1958. The estimate formed the basis for a sense of alarm in Washington that would only get worse. In fact, in Saudi Arabia Dulles' warning would prove prescient. On March 24, 1958, the royal family convened in Riyadh and took away Saud's powers on internal, foreign, and financial issues. He was effectively stripped of his powers, and they were given to his half-brother Crown Prince Faisal. Faisal had persuaded the family not to force Saud to abdicate but to simply give up control of the Kingdom. Saud would remain king, but Faisal would rule. Radio Mecca announced that Saud was leaving for Switzerland.[20]

Washington was deeply alarmed by Saud's departure and concerned about Faisal. On March 27 Dulles briefed the NSC on the changes in Riyadh. He expressed concern that Faisal "will arrange some kind of tie-up with Syria and Egypt," in effect joining the Nasser camp. But Dulles also provided a brief character sketch of Faisal that said he was not anti-American and was "definitely anti-communist." Vice President Richard Nixon described Faisal as "pro-American and smart as hell." Ike recalled that Faisal had been "extremely pleasant in his contacts in Washington."[21] The CIA was instructed to assess the implications of the change in Saudi Arabia.

In April, the intelligence community provided a Special National Intelligence Estimate (SNIE) titled "Implications of Recent Governmental Changes in Saudi Arabia" to the White House.[22] The SNIE reviewed the events of the so-called "Sarraj affair," the coup plot in Syria named for the former Syrian intelligence chief who produced the checks implicating King Saud. The affair and its resulting demotion of Saud was seen as "a victory for Nasserism and a repudiation of Saud's open anti-Nasser, pro-West policy." Faisal was expected to take a more "neutral" posture in inter-Arab affairs and avoid open disputes with the UAR and Nasser. This would find favor in the Saudi "Egyptianized army officer corps" and with the "Hejazi merchant community."[23]

Nonetheless, the SNIE also noted that Faisal would be a "traditional Saudi prince" and was determined to retain Saudi independence from Nasser. It noted Faisal supported the Dhahran Airfield Agreement of April 2, 1957, which kept the U.S. Air Force in the Kingdom. The chief impact of Saud's removal would be on Jordan, where Faisal was cutting financial subsidies to King Hussein and withdrawing Saudi troops from the country. The Estimate predicted that Faisal would practice "intense antagonism" toward Israel.[24] A few days after the SNIE was published, Dulles told the NSC that Faisal had told the base commander at Dhahran to cease flying the American flag at the base.[25]

The Syrian coup debacle was a turning point in 1958, a symbol of Nasser's growing prestige and power. The conservative camp in the Middle East was weakened, and Ike's protégé, Saud, was removed from the picture. It would take several more years before Saud abdicated, by which time Faisal had turned dramatically against Nasser. Saud moved to Cairo briefly, where he promoted propaganda against his brother and for his old nemesis before moving to Greece to live out the rest of his life.

The foiled coup strengthened Nasser's grip on Syria and removed his most powerful Arab opponent. It is a classic example of a covert action that ricocheted against its spy master. It further strengthened Nasser's image as the preeminent Arab leader of the time, who had vanquished America's chosen alternative and pushed its oldest ally toward neutrality in the inter-Arab cold war.

A straw in the wind came from a most unlikely corner. On March 8, 1958, the Mutawakkilite Kingdom of Yemen announced it was merging with the UAR. North Yemen was ruled by an almost medieval Zaydi Shia monarchy that was the very epitome of a corrupt, backward monarchy that Nasser had, allegedly, sought to destroy, but Yemen was a useful ally against two enemies for Nasser: Saudi Arabia and the British colony in southern Yemen around the port city of Aden. By creating a loose federation with the Yemeni monarchy, which kept its formal independence and its seat in the United Nations, Nasser had acquired a strategic arrow aimed at the Saudis, in case they became problematic, and at the most important port for the British Empire in the Indian Ocean.

The Yemeni alignment with Nasser helped buy off revolutionaries at home and provided some Arab nationalist legitimacy for the monarchy. It could appear more modern than it was. At the same time, Yemen acquired an ally against Saudi Arabia with which it had fought and lost a war in the 1930s, losing several border provinces along the way.

The Egyptian-Syrian-Yemeni confederation was called the United Arab States because Yemen was clearly not a republic. It added to the pressure on the Saudi royals to put Faisal in real power and further cemented the impression that Nasser was on the march and that he was an irresistible force, devouring the Arab states to form one grand state and drive the West from the Middle East. The changes in Riyadh and Sana'a made Washington very nervous.

Three

BEIRUT AND AMMAN

Beirut was commonly called "the Paris of the Middle East" in the 1950s and 1960s. It was the most cosmopolitan of all the cities in the Eastern Mediterranean and the Middle East and was known for the finest shopping, the finest restaurants, and the finest nightlife. It was also the intellectual capital of the region, home of the prestigious American University of Beirut (AUB). The Palestinian nationalist movement was born in Beirut and, especially, at AUB. Every political party in the Arab world had an office in Beirut, as did every significant newspaper from around the world.

It was also a center for espionage and diplomacy; every intelligence service that mattered was represented in Beirut. Plots and conspiracies were hatched and uncovered in a dizzy whirlwind of adventurers. The Lebanese government and its security service monitored this buzz of activity but rarely interfered unless it detected a threat to Lebanon's own independence.

The tiny country, smaller than the size of Connecticut, is blessed with a beautiful coastline and magnificent mountains just beyond the beaches. You can ski in the morning and swim in the afternoon, or the other way around. Tourists in the 1950s flocked to the city, as did bankers and financiers, confident their money was safe. Its airport was connected to everywhere and was the *entrée* to the entire region, and Beirut was the place to make a deal in the Middle East.

The Christian community—especially its largest component, the Maronites—spoke French and insisted on their European identity. The French had intervened in Lebanon since the Crusades and developed a close bond with the Maronites. Because of the French colonial period, the Maronites ran the country. The Muslim community was divided between Sunni, Shia, and Druze, with a handful of Alawites, and each community tended to live apart from the others, although segregation was not as stark and complete as it is today. The country prided itself as a model for democracy, diversity, and inclusion.

We now know that it could not and would not last. By the mid-1970s, Lebanon had descended into a hellish civil war and had become the battlefield of the Arab-Israeli conflict; numerous states supported local militias to score proxy victories over each other. Beirut would be the center

King Faisal of Iraq and
King Hussein of Jordan.

of the storm and would become a divided city with an ugly, violent frontline down its center. The banks and the tourists would leave, and the spies would stay. The crisis of 1958, in retrospect, can be seen as a trial run for Lebanon's coming agonies.

My family moved from Jerusalem to Beirut before the crisis of 1958 began. My father was a professional officer with the United Nations, which he had joined after its secretariat was set up following the Second World War. He had enlisted in the U.S. Army Air Force in the war, served in Algeria and Italy, and used the GI Bill to get an education, including a master's degree from Columbia University. Then president of Columbia University, Dwight David Eisenhower, signed his diploma.

Camille Chamoun

Modern Lebanon is a product of French imperialism. France has had an interest in the area and the Maronite community dating from the Crusades. In the nineteenth century, Paris forced the Ottoman Empire to give it special status in the Maronite Christian-dominated area around Beirut called Mount Lebanon. France claimed Lebanon and Syria after World War I and expanded the size of Mount Lebanon at Syria's expense. The original Mount Lebanon entity was 4,500 square kilometers; the expanded Lebanon is 10,450 square kilometers. By creating a larger Lebanon, the French brought many more Muslims into the state. In 1921, the Christians were estimated to be 53.4 percent of the population.[1]

Between the two world wars, the French cultivated the Maronite community. French is the language of educated Maronites, and, as one expert notes, Lebanese nationalism is "essentially Christian, viewing Lebanon as the 'national home'—very much under Maronite leadership of Lebanese Christians of all denominations."[2] Maronite Christians dominated the political scene after independence from France in 1946.

The president of Lebanon in 1958 was Camille Nimr Chamoun, sometimes spelled Shamun, and he was the most enthusiastic backer of the Eisenhower Doctrine in the Arab world. Chamoun was born April 3, 1900, into a prominent Maronite family in Mount Lebanon, the Christian heartland north and east of Beirut, still in the Ottoman Empire. He studied at Saint Joseph University and was first elected to the Parliament in 1934, then was re-elected in 1937 and 1943.

Chamoun was a Lebanese nationalist and a defender of Maronite rights in Lebanon for his entire political life. His two sons, Dany and Dory, carry on that tradition. His political career was all about protecting Lebanese sovereignty and ensuring Maronite Christian dominance within the Lebanese state, and he was an early proponent of independence from France after France was defeated by Germany in 1940. In November 1943, he was arrested and imprisoned, along with Bishara al Khoury and Riad al Solh—who would go on to become the first president and first prime minister, respectively, of the country—for agitating for independence. Mass public protests followed, and they all were released on November 22, 1943, a date that has since become the nation's independence day.

Khoury and Solh were also both from notable families. They were the drafters of the National Pact in 1943 that designed the unique political system of Lebanon that distributes power with a Maronite Christian president, a Sunni Muslim prime minister, and a Shia Muslim speaker of the parliament. Their self-proclaimed goal was to "Arabize the Christians" and "Lebanonize the Muslims." In other words, the Maronites would accept that they were not French Europeans but, in fact, Christian Arabs who spoke French surrounded by Muslims with whom they had to compromise, while the Muslims would accept that Lebanon could not become just another Arab Muslim state and must remain independent. Tolerance was their goal.[3]

Chamoun became Lebanon's ambassador to the United Kingdom in 1944 and then ambassador to the United Nations in 1946. With these assignments, he became a prominent figure on the world stage and in Lebanese political culture.

The 1948 war between Israel and its Arab neighbors was perceived as a threat to Maronite independence because it aroused pan-Arab sentiments to the cause of the Palestinian people, and Christians were afraid they would be submerged in a much larger Arab Muslim world. Consequently, Lebanon paid only lip service to the Arab Palestinian cause next door and sent no troops to fight Israel. Israel did occupy several Lebanese villages along the border but returned them in the armistice of 1949.[4]

The war resulted in 150,000 Arab Palestinians fleeing into Lebanon from Galilee. Most were Sunni Muslims, and this upset the delicate demographic balance in the country. As a result, the Palestinians were not made Lebanese citizens, and most lived in squalid refugee camps. Many still do. Higher Muslim, especially Shia, birth rates also upset the balance. By 1958, Christians were probably no longer a majority, but the pretense of their dominance was preserved by the absence of any census of the country's sectarian demographics.

In 1952, Chamoun was elected president, replacing Bishara al Khoury. Chamoun owed his election both to Christians, especially the Maronite Phalange Party, and Muslims, especially the Druze leader Kamal Junblatt. Chamoun's win tilted the country toward the United States. Though initially cautious not to get caught up in the rivalries between the larger Arab states, Chamoun's caution lasted only a couple of years.

As in Jordan, 1955 was a turning point for Lebanon. Chamoun traveled to Turkey in April, and the Turkish president made a return visit to Beirut in June. Turkey was a member of both the Baghdad Pact and NATO, and the two visits were widely interpreted as a sign Lebanon was going to join the Baghdad Pact. Syria, Egypt, and Saudi Arabia all worried that Chamoun was moving into Iraq's corner.[5]

The Suez Crisis the next year accelerated the divisions, led by Nasser, between Chamoun and the Arab states. Alone among the Arab states, Lebanon took no action against England and France for invading Egypt. Egypt, Syria, and Saudi Arabia broke relations with both countries, while Iraq and Jordan broke ties with France alone. Sunni Prime Minister Abdallah al Yafi resigned in protest from Chamoun's government.[6]

On March 16, 1957, Chamoun's government formally accepted the Eisenhower Doctrine as applying to the defense of Lebanon. A United National Front was created in protest and to oppose the Chamounists. It's three leading figures were two Sunni politicians (Yafi and Saib Salam) and the leader of the Druze community Kamal Junblatt. Junblatt was a traditional notable who was a large land owner. But the Front also was supported by many Christians, including, most notably, the Maronite Patriarch, the leader of the Church. So the 1958 crisis was not just a Christian versus Muslim confrontation but a more complex struggle over the identity of the nation.

Nasser escalated his withering propaganda against Chamoun. He accused Chamoun of having secret contacts with Israel (with good reason). More important, he accused him of being a puppet of the United States and Iraq.

Parliamentary elections were held in the spring, with a sweeping and implausible victory for the Chamoun government. The president's supporters won over two-thirds of the seats in the chamber, and the three leaders of the United National Front lost their seats despite being extremely popular in the Sunni and Druze communities. The results were immediately contested, and the Front refused to recognize the results as legitimate.[7]

Chamoun was forgetting the lessons of Khoury and Solh about tolerance. The late Lebanese historian Fouad Ajami wrote of Chamoun as follows: "He threw caution to the wind, sought an alliance with the U.S., with the conservative Arab monarchies of Iraq and Jordan against the radical tide of Arab nationalism. He carelessly rigged a national election to oust his opponents to get himself reelected."[8]

Chamoun had won with outside money. The Iraqi government was one source; the United States another. Egypt increased its attacks on Chamoun, and its embassy in Beirut became a bastion of the opposition.

The merger of Egypt and Syria in February 1958 vastly increased the passion of Arab nationalism in Lebanon. Schools closed around the country to celebrate the union, and tens of thousands of Lebanese Muslims traveled to Damascus to cheer for Nasser and the UAR. The opposition leadership met with the Egyptian leader in Syria. One expert account says 350,000 Lebanese made the pilgrimage to Damascus to pay homage to Nasser and signal their support for Arab unity. This is a remarkable number, as the nation's total population was only 1.5 million at the time. [9]

"The birth of the UAR and Nasser's visit to Damascus, indirectly and without prior intention, helped bring the Lebanese crisis to a head," according to the best researched account of the civil war in 1958.[10] The massive wave of popular support among the Muslims for the UAR reinforced the deep fears of the Maronite community that Lebanon's independence was at risk. To gain Western, especially American, support, they portrayed Nasser and the UAR as tools of international communism and the Soviet Union.

It was an easy sell with Secretary Dulles and Eisenhower, who were increasingly inclined to believe the worst about Nasser. The Lebanese president told the American, British, and French ambassadors that he was determined to fight the Nasserist menace and he would amend the Lebanese constitution to allow himself to run for reelec-

tion, which the National Pact forbade. Chamoun never announced in public his intention to run again, but it became
the issue that ignited the 1958 Lebanese civil war. The
Muslims and many Christians were completely opposed to
an illegal second term.

The spark that set off the civil war was the assassination of a leading Maronite journalist Nassib al Matani on
May 8, 1958. Matani was a major critic of Chamoun and
a supporter of the UAR, despite being a Maronite himself,
and he received numerous death threats from the president's loyalists before being killed.[11]

The United National Front called for a general strike
to protest the assassination and demanded Chamoun
immediately resign, but the president isolated himself
in the presidential residence in Beirut. The strike set off
violence, beginning in the northern city of Tripoli, then
Druze leader Junblatt organized an attack on the other
presidential palace in Bayt al Din outside Beirut and the
country split in two.

The rebels controlled most of the country, including
western, mostly Muslim, Beirut, most of Tripoli, and all
of Sidon, the country's three largest cities. The eastern
half of the country around the Biqa Valley was also in
rebel hands, as was almost all of the south and far north.
Chamoun's supporters held on to East Beirut and Mount
Lebanon, the territory just northeast of the capital and the
homeland of the Maronites. In all, the Chamoun government controlled less than 30 percent of the nation by July
1958.[12]

The rebels were a loosely organized collection of militias. The most powerful and best led was Kamal Junblatt's Druze. They led the attacks on Christian strongholds, including the largest attack on East Beirut, in early July 1958. That offensive ended in a stalemate, and the Christians hung on to East Beirut. The Muslims held the West, including the district known as the Basta, which was a Sunni stronghold.

The government's strongest loyal force was the Phalange Party. The Phalange was created in 1936 after a visit by its founder and leader Pierre Jumayyil to Nazi Germany. Jumayyil was impressed by the Nazi party and, especially, by its leader Adolf Hitler. He created the Phalange as a fascist party complete with all the symbols of fascism. By 1958, it had 40,000 members, all Christians, all well trained and totally committed to a Maronite Lebanon.[13] The Phalange also had been secretly working with Israel sporadically since 1948, as both opposed Arab nationalists.[14]

Another key supporter was the Syrian nationalist party known as the PPS, or Syrian Popular Party. They were supporters of a united Syria but not a united Arab nation. Banned in Syria, the PPS chose Lebanon as its base. Much smaller than the Phalange, the PPS was effectively a terrorist organization, and was responsible for Riad al Solh's assassination in 1951.

Both sides got support—including money, men, and arms—from the outside. The UAR backed the rebels and used the long and unprotected border with Syria to smuggle aid to the Muslims, especially to Junblatt, whose power base was in the Shuf region southeast of Beirut. Iraq was the main supplier to the government.

The Lebanese army stayed neutral during the war. Its commander, a French-trained officer from a powerful Maronite family, General Fuad Shihab, was a Maronite, but he had longstanding friendships with all the Muslim rebel leaders. All the leaders on both sides were like Shihab; that is, members of the establishment who were beneficiaries of Lebanon's system, not radical street fighters.

Shihab was not a Chamounist, and he was against amending the constitution to allow a second term. He also feared, correctly, that if the army intervened in the civil war, it would fragment and collapse, as it did, in fact, in the 1970s. While the officer corps was mostly Christian, the enlisted ranks included many Muslims, particularly Shia.

Washington followed the decline into civil war and *de facto* partition with growing concern. Chamoun asked for American and British intervention to defeat the rebels, but Eisenhower held back. He was reluctant in general to send American troops into combat. After all, he knew more than most the costs of war. Eisenhower had been elected to end the war in Korea, and though he liked Chamoun very much and was worried about Nasser, he recognized the civil war was a complex affair and not a black-and-white case; at least not so far.

In late June, the CIA sent Miles Copeland to Cairo for a secret consultation with Nasser about Lebanon. According to Copeland's account, Nasser said that "if the solution were entirely up to him, he would make General Shihab President and Rashid Karami Prime Minister." In turn, Egypt would accept Lebanon's neutrality.[15]

The United Nations was called into action by its dynamic secretary general, the Swedish diplomat Dag Hammarskjold. On June 11, 1958, at the secretary general's suggestion, the Security Council created the United Nations Observation Group in Lebanon (UNOGIL) to monitor the civil war, in general, and, specifically, to report on outside intervention and arms assistance to the parties. The council voted ten in favor with one abstention, from Russia, to set up the observers. This took some time, but by July, UNOGIL had about 500 personnel on the ground, including my father.

UNOGIL had an impossible mission. The rebels controlled nearly all the border region and would allow inspection only under their supervision. Three-quarters of the country were effectively in their hands. UN inspectors were allowed in rebel territory only in daylight hours and only with advance permission. UNOGIL did acquire aircraft and helicopters to allow aerial supervision, but this was difficult to do, especially at night. The geography was simply too big for the UN force. UNOGIL's reports to the Security Council openly acknowledged its limitations. They did not find evidence of large-scale UAR support to the rebels.

Eisenhower was a prudent planner, and he authorized military preparation for an intervention in Lebanon as the civil war developed. U.S. forces in the Mediterranean Sea, the Sixth Fleet with its accompanying Marines, would be the first to act, backed by the large American military force in Western Europe. The Pentagon coordinated closely with the British. Washington and London agreed on a separation of responsibility; both countries placed forces on alert and sent in reinforcements. If the crisis boiled over, the Americans would handle Lebanon and the British Jordan.

Hussein bin Talal

No one in the Middle East in 1958 would confuse Amman with Paris. The sleepy backwater of the Arab world, Amman was the capital of the Hashemite Kingdom of Jordan. Founded on the ruins of the ancient city of Philadelphia, it was chosen for the capital by Abdallah bin Hashem, the founder of the Kingdom, in 1921. Abdallah had been a commander in the Arab revolt against the Ottoman Turks in the First World War, which was led by his father, the Sharif of Mecca. When the war ended and the Ottoman Empire was dissolved, Britain took control of Palestine, including Trans Jordan and Iraq. The Hashemites were driven out of Mecca and the Hejaz by the Saudis.

The British sought to reward their Hashemite allies and stabilize their most important new possession by placing Abdallah's older brother, Faisal, on the throne in oil rich Iraq. Anxious to find a place for Abdallah, Britain's minister for colonial affairs Winston Churchill convened a meeting in Cairo in 1921 to draw the borders of Britain's empire. Churchill took Trans Jordan out of the Palestine mandate and gave it to Abdallah as the Emirate of Trans Jordan. With his retinue of mostly Hejazi supporters, Abdallah and his British aides set up the emirate's capital in Amman.

Abdallah faced enormous obstacles. Most of the East Bank is desert. The economy was primitive and the infrastructure almost nonexistent. Abdallah was an ambitious man who aspired to govern more than the "vacant lot," as some British diplomats called Trans Jordan. He especially was eager to acquire Syria, but that was a daunting task. Abdallah did acquire the West Bank and East Jerusalem in the 1948 war thanks to the military skills of Glubb Pasha and the Arab Legion, assisted behind the scenes by some clandestine diplomatic contacts with Israel. The union of the West Bank with Trans Jordan created the Hashemite Kingdom of Jordan. Most of the world did not formally recognize Jordanian sovereignty in the West Bank and Jerusalem; only Great Britain and Pakistan did. The population was two-thirds, 900,000, Palestinian and one-third, 450,000, East Bankers or Trans Jordanians.[16]

Abdallah's close ties to London and rumors of his back channel to Israel made him very unpopular among his new Palestinian citizens. On July 20, 1951, the king was assassinated outside the Al Aqsa mosque in Jerusalem by an assassin with contacts with the extremists in the Palestinian community. Only four days earlier, Lebanese Prime Minister Riad al Solh had been assassinated in Amman. Riad al Solh was perhaps the most prominent Arab critic of Abdallah's clandestine connections with Israel. Some believe Solh was lured to Jordan by Abdallah to have him assassinated by the Syrian nationalist party, possibly even with Israeli collusion.[17] Solh's murder aroused intense Arab nationalist sentiments against the king. Both the British and American ambassadors in Amman warned the king that Jerusalem was not safe, but Abdallah was in Jerusalem to meet secretly with Israeli envoys.[18]

Prince Hussein bin Talal, the king's favorite grandson, was standing by his side. The assassin put his pistol to the king's ear and fired a single shot, which killed Abdallah instantly. The assassin fired a shot at Hussein, as well, but it ricocheted off a medal his grandfather had insisted he wear that day.[19]

After Abdallah's assassination, his son Talal ascended to the throne. Talal, who suffered from mental illness, was regarded as an interim figure until his son Hussein was old enough to rule. Hussein moved to the throne in 1952, but, as noted in an earlier chapter, he faced a serious challenge to his survival during the Baghdad Pact riots in December 1955 and January 1956. He survived only by resorting to use of the Royal Jordanian Army, led by Glubb Pasha, and then dismissed Glubb only a few months later.

In October 1956, parliamentary elections brought to power the National Socialist Party led by Suleiman al Nabulsi, an Arab nationalist sympathetic to Nasser. In March 1957, Nabulsi abrogated the Anglo-Jordan Treaty, which had committed the United Kingdom to the defense of Jordan and provided an annual financial stipend for the Kingdom. This was a challenge to both London and Hussein. The next month, Hussein fired Nabulsi and dissolved parliament.

The king faced a military mutiny in April 1957. According to his version of events, he discovered that the army chief of staff was planning a move on Amman to take power for the nationalists. The king took off to visit the rebellious troops with the arrested suspect chief of staff in the back seat of a Chevrolet. At the cantonment of Zarqa, eleven miles from Amman, the king confronted his troops directly and demanded their loyalty. At great personal risk, Hussein prevailed, and the army proclaimed its loyalty to its sovereign. Syria had been poised to intervene to help the rebels, but held back when it saw the king had turned the tide.[20] These dramatic events added to the luster of the king's image as "the plucky little king," and Hussein soon announced his implicit endorsement of the Eisenhower Doctrine.

Washington and London realized that Hussein's rule was still precarious. Contingency planning began between the American and British military leadership for a possible intervention in Jordan in the spring of 1957.[21] This planning would evolve in time into the twin operations conducted in July 1958: the Marine landing in Beirut and the British paratrooper intervention in Amman.

The king reorganized his army in the wake of the foiled coup. Units composed of Bedouin tribesmen from the East Bank were installed in all key facilities, while Palestinians were segregated out of the officer corps of the army. The nascent intelligence service became the exclusive preserve of East Bank loyalists.

In March 1958, Jordan became the junior partner in the new Arab Federation. It was not a popular move in Jordan. Those who favored Arab unity were much more impressed by the UAR and Nasser. Palestinians were unenthusiastic about King Faisal II as their new commander, and the country was still under martial law imposed after the failed April 1957 coup.

Another coup plot was in the works; this one was uncovered in Washington, not in the Middle East. The Federal Bureau of Investigation (FBI) tapped the phone of the Jordanian deputy chief of mission in the American capital. Major General Mahmud Rusen was in conspiracy with his Egyptian counterpart. The tapes showed Rusen was the central player in a coup plot to kill King Hussein and overthrow the Jordanian monarchy, breaking up the Arab Federation, with the support of Egyptian intelligence. Rusen had served earlier in Washington as the military attaché.

For many years, it was believed Israel was the ultimate source of the information on the 1958 plot, but it was, in fact, the CIA, as was unveiled in 2011 by the CIA officer who took the information to Amman and briefed the king, Jack O'Connell.[22] O'Connell gave the king enough information to persuade him to recall Rusen to Amman where his activities could be closely monitored. The surveillance uncovered a cell of twenty-two Jordanian officers involved in the plot.[23]

In late June 1958, according to O'Connell's first-hand account, the CIA intercepted a message from the Egyptian service in Syria ordering the coup plotters to proceed immediately with the king's assassination and the coup. The king had all twenty-two plotters arrested immediately, and they confessed.

The arrest of the plotters was a vivid illustration for both the Americans and British that Jordan was at severe risk from the UAR. The plot had been organized by Nasser's henchman in Damascus, Abdel Hamid Sarraj, the same person who had uncovered the Saud plot in 1958 to assassinate Nasser that led to the downfall of King Saud.[24]

On July 10, 1958, Iraqi army commander General Rafiq Arif came to Amman on the instructions of King Faisal II to warn Hussein that Nasser was plotting against him. In turn, King Hussein told Arif that Jordan had information that two senior Iraqi officers, Brigadier General Abdul Karim Kassem and Colonel Ab al Salam Arif, were plotting to overthrow Faysal. The two had been stationed in Jordan the year before, when Jordanian intelligence first detected their conspiracy. The Iraqi army had stationed a brigade in northern Jordan since the Baghdad Pact riots to help the king keep his throne and deter Syrian intervention across the border. The Iraqi army chief dismissed the allegations and returned to Baghdad.

Hussein also asked the Iraqis to send an additional brigade of troops to help back up his government. In response, Iraqi Prime Minister Nuri al Said decided to send the Twentieth Brigade Group, based east of Baghdad, to

Jordan. The brigade was to move through Baghdad *en route* to Jordan on the night of July 13, 1958.

By the middle of July 1958, two small states, Lebanon and Jordan, were seemingly at risk of moving out of the orbit of the West and toward Nasser. In Lebanon, a civil war was underway. Washington was still shaken by the loss of King Saud as Ike's alternative to Nasser, and the Egyptian leader seemed to have outfoxed the president time and time again. Eisenhower and his team were anxious.

Four

BAGHDAD AND WASHINGTON

The phone rang in the communicator's bedroom just before four in the morning on July 14, 1958. John and his wife had arrived in April in Iraq after a tour of duty in Beirut. (John served in the intelligence community and his full name is classified.) The call was from his boss in the embassy in Baghdad. John was urgently needed to open the communications office to send messages to Washington. Communicators had an unglamorous but crucial role in the world of diplomacy and espionage. They ensured that coded messages moved back and forth from missions all over the world. They spent long hours at work and could be called in at a moment's notice, even when the embassy was closed.

A car picked John up, and he heard gunfire as they

drove to the embassy. Later in the morning, he brought his wife by car to the embassy, as well, for her safety. Two days later, she was evacuated from the country; it was the most frightening moment in their career. Along the highway to the airport, dead bodies of regime loyalists hung from the street lights. John and his wife worried they would be killed at any moment, and in fact, some Western businessmen were assassinated. John would leave Baghdad in December, just six months after his arrival.[1]

The July 14, 1958, coup had come as a complete surprise to Washington and London. Both the United States and the United Kingdom had long suspected the monarchy might be vulnerable to a coup, but neither had any warning of the crisis when it arrived.[2]

Modern Iraq, like Trans Jordan, was Winston Churchill's creation. In 1921, at the Cairo conference where he created the Emirate of Trans Jordan for Abdallah, Churchill had stitched together three provinces of the former Ottoman Empire—Basra, Baghdad, and Mosul—into a new country, to be named either Mesopotamia or Iraq. The borders were drawn, for the most part, with straight lines, and Faisal I was made king.[3] He had never visited Iraq before, and when he arrived at Basra on June 24, 1921, to take up his throne, there was no one to meet him. Only empty train stations greeted him, all the way to Baghdad. It was an inauspicious start.[4]

The British gave Iraq independence in 1932. Faisal died in 1933 and was succeeded by a weak son, Ghazi, who held the throne until his own death in a car accident in 1939.

Faisal II, Ghazi's son, born in 1935, was underage, so a cousin, Abdallah, ruled as regent until Faisal II came of age in 1953. During the second world war, a military coup briefly installed a pro-German government in 1941, and the British invaded Iraq to prevent the military regime from allying the country with Nazi Germany. The Arab Legion played a part in that invasion, and Rashid Ali, the pro-Nazi Iraqi politician, fled to Saudi Arabia. During the military regime, Abdallah lived in exile in Amman.

After the war, in late 1945, Abdallah visited the United States and was feted at the White House at Harry Truman's first state dinner as president. The regent toured Mount Vernon, the first U.S. president's home, in Virginia. But the Kingdom's main patron remained the United Kingdom, which relied on Iraq as the centerpiece of the Baghdad Pact.

Iraq is deeply divided along both ethnic and sectarian lines. A majority of Iraqis are Arabs, but there is a substantial Kurdish minority in the north that has never been comfortable being ruled by Arabs. The Arab majority is divided between a Sunni minority and a Shia majority. The Shia live primarily south of Baghdad and the Sunnis to the west; the center of the country is mixed. The Arab Sunni minority was put in charge of running the region during the Ottoman Empire, which was also Sunni, and the British perpetuated Sunni rule. The Hashemites are also Sunni.

The country was backward and corrupt. A land-owning aristocracy possessed almost everything of value. Two-thirds of Iraqi agricultural lands belonged to a handful of land owners; only 15 percent of the land was possessed by the farmers who actually farmed the land. The bulk of the population lived in "virtual serfdom."[5] The country was ripe for revolution.

The July 14 Revolution

Faisal II was only twenty-three years old in 1958. The former regent and now crown prince, Abdallah still exercised considerable influence on the king, but the most influential figure was Prime Minister Nuri al Said. The crown prince "was not particularly bright, not at all able, rather lazy and lacking in any social graces," according to one of King Hussein's biographers. "Said was the real mover and shaker and the supreme manipulator of Iraqi politics." Glubb Pasha recalled that Nuri once told him that "a dog could not bark in Baghdad without Nuri hearing of it."[6]

Born in 1888, Nuri served as prime minister in Iraq fourteen times, starting in 1930. He was the preeminent fixture of Iraqi politics for almost three decades, and above all, Nuri was a defender of Iraq's close relationship with the British.

He was born to a middle-class family in Baghdad, of Turkmen origin, and went to Istanbul to study in the military academy. He served with the Ottoman army in Libya beginning in 1912, fighting the Italians. In 1915, he was captured by the British and held prisoner in Egypt, where he converted to the cause of Arab nationalism and the Hashemite-led Arab revolt against the Turks. He served with the future King Faisal and the famous T. E. Lawrence of Arabia. Nuri led the capture of Damascus in 1918, and in the 1920s, he built Iraq's new police force and army, creating his own power base loyal to him and the Hashemite monarchy.

In his first stint as prime minister, Nuri signed the 1930 Anglo-Iraq Treaty, which confirmed London's mandatory power. During a brief coup in 1936, Nuri fled to the British embassy and then took exile in Cairo, Britain's stronghold. Iraqi politics in the late 1930s were a confusing series of plots and conspiracies in which Nuri's position rose and fell. King Ghazi, Faisal's successor, died in a car crash in April 1939, and Nuri was widely suspected of a role in the accident, though never charged. He became Regent Abdallah's chief advisor, then fled again to Cairo in 1941 during the brief military regime backed by the Nazis. He returned later with the British army and was made prime minister by the British.

In the 1950s, Nuri was the architect of Iraqi policy at home and abroad. He was behind the Baghdad Pact and Iraq's close alliance with Britain. The 1956 Suez Crisis was a grave setback for his fortunes. There were massive protests in Baghdad, Basra, and other Iraqi cities against the Anglo-French-Israeli invasion of Egypt, and the police and army suppressed them violently. Iraq broke ties with France but not with England. Nuri was "increasingly out of touch with the bulk of Iraqi opinion" as Nasser's charisma grew. The 1956 crisis rendered "Nuri more un-popular than ever in Iraq: long known as Britain's crony, he was now branded also as the dupe of an ally that had fought alongside Israel."[7]

Neither Abdallah nor Nuri al Said were entirely eager about the union in February 1958 with Jordan. Jordan was much poorer than Iraq, and the large Palestinian popula-tion was considered disloyal. Nuri was particularly eager that Kuwait join the federation to help defray the costs of bucking up Jordan, but the British, who still ruled Kuwait, were against the idea of adding Kuwait. In the end, the reluctant Iraqis accepted the need to create an alternative to the UAR. Nuri pressed for Kuwait to join the union right up to the coup that toppled him from office.[8]

The Arab Federation was launched February 14, 1958, Valentine's Day in the United States, with much celebra-tion. The flag of the Arab Revolt in World War I—black, red, white, and green—was flown. King Hussein broad-cast to the nation that "this is the happiest day of my life, a great day in Arab history." Faisal gave an enthusiastic speech, as well.[9] Nuri was named prime minister for the federation.

A Free Officers movement was created in Iraq after the Egyptian coup in 1952 that put Nasser in power. The Egyp-tian example inspired Lieutenant Colonel Salih Abd al Majid al Samarrai, then Iraq's defense attaché in Amman, to set up the clandestine cell. Others gradually joined the first cell, including, in 1954, Colonel Abd al Karim

Iraqi Prime Minister
Abd al Karim Qassem.

Qassem. By 1958, the conspiracy had grown to include an estimated 150 officers.[10]

Qassem was born December 21, 1914, in a poor quarter of Baghdad, to a Sunni Arab father and a Shia Kurdish mother. In 1932, he entered military college and graduated two years later. He participated in the war against the British invasion in 1941. He did not come under fire himself, but did serve as a battalion commander with the Iraqi army expeditionary corps that went to Palestine in 1948. He was stationed fifteen miles east of Tel Aviv and remained there until June 1949. In 1956 and 1957, he was stationed with the Iraqi army brigade in northern Jordan just south of the Syria border at Mafraq. He never married.[11] Qassem also was a favorite of Crown Prince Abdallah, or at least he pretended to be his loyal supporter.[12]

With the CIA's information about a Syrian-Egyptian coup plot, King Hussein asked Baghdad to send another brigade to Jordan to help preserve the monarchy and the federation. The government chose the Twentieth Brigade, which was stationed ninety miles east of Baghdad, toward the border with Iran. The plan called for the brigade to transit through the capital on the night of July 13 on its way to Faluja and then on to Jordan. The Royal Guards and the Ministry of Interior were not informed of the planned move, which was regarded as routine. Usually troops moving through Baghdad had no ammunition, but these troops were fully armed and equipped.

The royal family was distracted by two major events. First, King Faisal was to be married in October. His bride-to-be was studying English, hurriedly, in London, and planning for the wedding was consuming much of the king's time. Second, he was due to travel to Turkey on the morning of July 14 for a Baghdad Pact summit meeting. The regent had just returned from a preliminary meeting in Ankara.[13]

At three in the morning of July 14, Colonel Abd al Salam Aref took command of the lead battalion of the brigade. Like Qassem, Aref was a member of the Free Officers movement. Under his command, the battalion seized control of the Ministry of Defense and the radio office of the government by four o'clock. The Royal Palace was surrounded by five a.m., with the king and the crown prince, as well as many of the members of the royal family, inside. The rest of the brigade took control of the city.

Hopelessly isolated from the rest of the country, the king surrendered the palace at seven thirty in the morning. Faisal II, Abdallah, Princess Nafissa, the widow of King Ali, and Princess Abadiya, the king's aunt, were placed against a wall in the palace courtyard and machine gunned to death. Only Princess Hiyam, who had hidden inside the palace, survived the massacre. She later fled to the Saudi embassy and survived.[14] As Elizabeth Monroe notes, "King Faisal II and the British alliance were consumed in the holocaust; the statue of Faisal I was dragged in the dust."[15]

Later in the morning, Baghdad radio announced that Brigadier General Qassem was the new head of state and had established his headquarters in the Defense Ministry. Baghdad radio praised Gamal Abd al Nasser, and his photo was placed on the rebels' tanks. King Faisal Street was renamed for Nasser.[16] Crowds soon formed and chanted his name as they tore down the statues of Faisal I and General Frederick Stanley Maude, the commander of the British army who captured Baghdad from the Turks in 1917. Prime Minister Nuri al Said was in hiding, and the crowd grew increasingly unruly and attacked the British embassy.[17] The bodies of the king and crown prince were dragged through the streets and mutilated; Abdallah was beheaded.

Several foreign businessmen, including two Americans, were dragged from their hotels and killed. Nuri was found the day after the coup and murdered immediately, and his body mutilated. The corpse was dragged through the streets by a car. The British embassy in Baghdad was attacked by a mob, pillaged, and partially burned, and the British ambassador and his wife were detained by Iraqi soldiers for several hours before being sent to a hotel.[18]

The American embassy sent Washington its appraisal of the situation late in the day. Stressing that it had little direct information because of the danger to embassy personnel traveling outside the embassy compound, the mission reported "local enthusiasm for the coup is considerable" and there was "no sign yet of counter move spearheaded by any loyalist forces." Most important, the embassy said the "character of the coup is strongly anti-western and pro-Nasser. Crowds have been shouting pro-Nasser slogans and carrying Nasser's pictures." It also reported the deaths of the two American businessmen, Eugene Burns and George Colley Jr., from the Bechtel Corporation. The embassy was unaware of the fate of the king and the prime minister.[19] Other missions in Baghdad reported similar fragments of information. The coup plotters were largely unknown.

In Amman, King Hussein was told of the coup at seven in the morning. He learned then that his cousin Faisal was dead. They had been "the best of friends: they were born the same year, and were at Harrow together and they became kings on the same day," as one Israeli biographer recalled. Hussein was not a fan of the crown prince, however, and he blamed Abdallah for not giving Faisal more say in the running of Iraq. Indeed, he "hated him with a passion."[20]

The king would later say July 14, 1958, was the worst day of his life because of the loss of his cousin. He reacted that day by asserting his claim to the throne of the union in the demise of Faisal II and ordered his uncle Sharif Nasser to send Jordanian forces to Baghdad to reverse the coup. After a few hours, when the success of Qassem's coup was clear, Sharif Nasser was ordered to retreat back to Jordan.[21]

Washington Panics

The news from Baghdad startled Washington as it awakened on Monday, July 14, 1958, several hours behind Iraqi time. Eisenhower later wrote, "I was shocked" by the news of the coup.[22] Indeed, the administration panicked when the news came in from Iraq. After months of watching Nasser steadily gain influence across the Middle East and seeing their candidate to out-match Nasser stripped of his powers in Saudi Arabia, the Eisenhower team immediately jumped to the worst-case estimate for understanding the events in Baghdad and pulled the trigger. Instead of waiting for events to be clarified, Ike sent in the Marines. It was the first time Americans were sent into combat in the Middle East, and it set the pattern for much of what followed.

Eisenhower also awoke to a message from Chamoun in Beirut. The Lebanese president, who had been pushing for American intervention for weeks, told Ambassador McClintock that "your government had consistently underestimated his warning of danger in the Middle East. Now developments in Baghdad had proved him right and the U.S. wrong" for procrastinating. He was even harsher in his criticism of Dag Hammarskjold for giving Nasser "carte blanche" to disrupt the region. He said he wanted American military intervention in Lebanon within forty-eight hours. Chamoun made similar representations to the British and French ambassadors.[23]

McClintock told Washington that he believed the situation in Lebanon did not warrant intervention. He acknowledged that the decision to intervene needed to be based on "broader intelligence and political and strategic considerations affecting the entire Middle East." But he said "so far as Lebanon alone is concerned, we cannot as of midday discern the need for so portentous a step."[24]

Allen Dulles gave Eisenhower the broader intelligence picture at a National Security Council meeting in the White House at 10:50 that morning. The director of central intelligence (DCI) began by noting that the embassy in Baghdad was surrounded by tanks and had little "independent reporting." The fate of King Faisal was unknown, but the regent was "torn limb from limb and carried through the streets." Dulles stressed that the coup was "taken by pro-Nasir elements led by young army officers and backed by the mob." He suggested the coup leaders were in conspiracy with Egypt. "Nasir placards are much in evidence and the crowds are cheering Nasir." Radio Cairo was hailing the coup.[25]

The director then turned to the regional reactions to the coup. He reiterated Chamoun's request for immediate American military intervention. Dulles said there was an "ominous quiet" in Beirut. In Jordan, he reminded the NSC that the CIA had "uncovered what appeared to be a well-advanced Army plot to overthrow" King Hussein, which had just been "nipped in the bud." The king had assumed the role of Supreme Commander of the Arab Federation, "a courageous act," but his fate "hangs in the balance." The Saudis, Kuwaitis, and other Arab monarchies are threatened by these events. "If the Iraq coup succeeds it seems almost inevitable that it will set up a chain reaction which will doom the pro-West governments of Lebanon and Jordan and Saudi Arabia, and raise grave problems for Turkey and Iran." Israel, Dulles predicted, would take over the West Bank "if Jordan falls to Nasir."[26]

It was a very bleak picture Allen Dulles painted for the president and his cabinet. The entire Middle East was about to fall into the hands of international communism through the mechanism of Gamal Abd al Nasser. The DCI was unequivocal that "the hand of Nasir has been clearly apparent." Those who had conducted the coup in Iraq were "clearly identified with the pro-Egyptian campaign." Allen Dulles did admit that the timing "seems a little out of gear" with Nasser in Yugoslavia visiting Marshal Tito, but his bottom line was that the United States was on the verge of losing its Arab allies.[27]

The president commented "that this is probably our last chance to do something in the area." The window for action was closing fast, he said, and "we must move." John Foster Dulles then provided a lengthy political analysis. As always, he began with the Soviets. Moscow would be the beneficiary of the fall of pro-American governments in the region. "If we do not respond to the call from Chamoun, we will suffer the decline and indeed the elimination of our influence from Indonesia to Morocco." While Dulles cautioned that intervention would provoke a backlash in some Arab states, on balance, he thought there was more to lose from "doing nothing," and "consequently we should send our troops into Iraq." With that, the president said that "it was clear in his mind that we must act, or get out of the Middle East entirely." Ike concluded: "to lose this area by inaction would be far worse than the loss of China" to communism.[28]

Instructions were immediately sent by the Pentagon to the U.S. command in Europe and the Sixth Fleet in the Mediterranean. Since planning had been underway for weeks, the Navy was ready to act quickly. The Marines were to go ashore the next day, July 15, 1958, at 3 p.m. Beirut time (nine in the morning in Washington). Operation Blue Bat was the code name for the attack.[29]

Eisenhower met with several senators and congressmen after the NSC meeting. They were more divided in their views. "Most skeptical of all was Senator Fulbright who seemed to doubt seriously that this crisis was Communist inspired," Eisenhower later noted in his memoirs.[30] Other Democratic senators were also "unusually critical" in the next few days. Senator Wayne Morse of Oregon lamented "the mixing of American blood with Arabian oil." The strongest voice was Massachusetts Senator John F. Kennedy, who criticized the administration for viewing the Middle East "almost exclusively in the context of the East West struggle" while underestimating the "cutting force of Arab nationalism." Washington, JFK argued, should begin "doing business with Nasser."[31]

The White House received more news from the region during the afternoon and evening of July 14. The ambassador in Jordan reported on an urgent meeting with King Hussein, indicating that Hussein said he had taken over command of the Arab Federation and was in the process of establishing contact with loyal Iraqi forces with the intent to join with them to "crush the rebellion." The king asked for immediate American assistance for oil to fuel the tanks of the army. Airlifting fuel was crucial, the king said, and the embassy agreed. Finally, the king urged Eisenhower to send troops to Beirut to save Chamoun. He did not ask for troops for himself, since the coup plot was already wrapped up with the CIA's help. (Hussein later pulled back his troops from advancing to Baghdad and changed his mind on the request for foreign help.)[32]

The American ambassador in Tel Aviv was urgently summoned to see Prime Minister David Ben Gurion in the evening, Israeli time. Ben Gurion was accompanied by Foreign Minister Golda Meir and several aides. The Israeli leader urged the United States to press "Turkey and Iran to crush the Iraqi rebellion in a couple of days." King Hussein, as the new head of the Arab Federation, could invite Turkey and Iran, as members of the Baghdad Pact, to invade Iraq and restore the monarchy with Hussein as leader. "Turkey and Iran can put out the fire if they are backed up by the US but it is imperative the US take the lead," Ben Gurion said; if not, then the "loss of the Middle East would be the worst blow to the West since World War II." In that case, "Israel will be virtually surrounded in mortal danger."[33]

The Israelis were by far the most ambitious ally consulted, probably because they would not have to do anything themselves. The Baghdad Pact members—Turkey, Iran, and Pakistan—were consulted quickly by the State Department, and none expressed any desire to intervene in Iraq. They did urge intervention in Lebanon. The Turks urged Washington to formally join the Baghdad Pact.[34]

The most important conversation Eisenhower had was with British Prime Minister Harold Macmillan, around six in the evening Washington time. The United Kingdom was a Baghdad Pact member and had a mutual defense agreement with Jordan, and London was completely startled by the coup. The embassy was ignorant of the plotters and "poorly informed." The ambassador was in a hotel because the embassy had been attacked. It was a "devastating blow to the whole system of security which successive British governments had built," as Macmillan's biographer later described. Iraq was the cornerstone of British policy in the Middle East and it had been shattered.[35]

Eisenhower told Macmillan that the Marines would land in Beirut the next day, and suggested the British be ready to move into Jordan to bolster "the little chap" there. Macmillan promised support for whatever Eisenhower decided to do in Lebanon. Ike said "I realize we are opening a Pandora's box here, but if we don't open it, I think it is disastrous."[36]

America did open the Pandora's box of war in the Middle East after a single meeting at the White House, where panicked officials acted on almost no information but felt they must "do something." What accounted for Eisenhower's rushed decision? The president's poll ratings were in a slump, dropping thirty points in the first few months of 1958 to his lowest standing in eight years. Eisenhower had appeared to react slowly to the Soviet's launch of the Sputnik rocket, and "the president was seen as too passive, inert, distracted, vague—in short, too old and worn out for the job," as one of his biographers later wrote. He had suffered a stroke in late 1957, and now he needed to display strength and decisiveness.[37]

But the decisive factor was surprise; surprise at the events in Baghdad, which seemed to augur a revolution throughout the Middle East against American interests, which led to a rush to judgment. Rather than waiting for the dust to settle, Eisenhower chose to act quickly, and he turned to the most available instrument at hand, the military, and this set the pattern for similar decisions in the future. Thankfully, as we see in the next chapter, Eisenhower's Pandora's box did not explode.

Five

BEIRUT, AMMAN, AND BAGHDAD

At three in the afternoon on July 15, 1958, the second battalion of the 2nd Marine Regiment, 1,700 men, came ashore ready for combat, weapons loaded. The Sixth Fleet had assembled an armada of over seventy warships in the Eastern Mediterranean to support the landings. Three United States Navy aircraft carriers, the USS *Essex*, USS *Wasp*, and USS *Saratoga*, provided air support.[1] The 82nd Airborne Division in the United States was put on alert to reinforce the Marines if needed, and another Marine regimental combat team was deployed from Okinawa to the Persian Gulf to defend Saudi Arabia and Kuwait.[2]

On the beach at the time of the landing were Lebanese and foreign tourists, some in bikinis, sunbathing or playing in the water. As the Marines stormed the beach, the sunbathers rushed to safety. Down the beach, Lebanese vendors of soft drinks, cigarettes, and sandwiches rushed to sell their wares to the newcomers. As the Marines settled in on the beach, Lebanese teenagers hurried to help them unload their equipment. Further away, the opposition prepared for battle.

America's first combat mission in the Middle East began with a combination of farce, comedy, and grave danger. My family saw the Marines come ashore as sniper fire in downtown Beirut kept the streets empty. We lived in an apartment in West Beirut, on the Muslim side of the city, close to the famous Pigeon Rocks, a grouping of tall rocks just offshore from West Beirut that was a must-take photo opportunity for every visitor to Lebanon.

It was a momentous day. For the first time ever, an American president had sent combat troops into a Middle Eastern country. No one could have foreseen that this day would be the start of decades of American wars in the region.

It was also an unusual day for President Dwight David Eisenhower, the only day in his eight years as president that he ordered troops into combat. Eisenhower, the greatest general in the country's greatest war, never served in combat himself, but he saw the results of war firsthand and often in World War II. As president, his top priority was to keep the peace. His biographer, Evan Thomas, argues persuasively in *Ike's Bluff* that Eisenhower was determined to use the threat of war, especially the threat of

*Camille Nemr Chamoun, second
president of Lebanon (1952–1958).*

nuclear war, to avoid actual combat and to keep the peace.
On July 15, Ike was threatening war in Lebanon.[3]

Shortly after the first troops came ashore, Eisenhower
addressed the nation from the Oval Office. He began by
discussing the events in Baghdad of July 14. It "was a day
of grave developments in the Middle East." The Iraqi monarchy was swept away "with great brutality" and grue-
some violence. In Jordan, Eisenhower said, "at about the
same time there was discovered a highly organized plot
to overthrow the lawful government" of King Hussein.
(This was somewhat misleading; the CIA had uncov-

ered the plot weeks before.) Then Eisenhower turned to the topic of Lebanon and told his listeners that President Chamoun had requested American military intervention to stop "civil strife" that was "actively fomented by Soviet and Cairo broadcasts" as well as by arms and personnel infiltrated into Lebanon from Syria. The reference to Cairo radio was the only time in the president's speech that he even alluded to Gamal Abd al Nasser, the United Arab Republic, or the Arab nationalist movement.[4]

Instead of discussing the Egyptian leader, Eisenhower spoke in Cold War terms. Lebanon, a country the size of Connecticut, with 1.5 million people, was under attack by the "same pattern of conquest with which we became familiar during the period of 1945 to 1950" when the "Communists" threatened Greece, took over Czechoslovakia and mainland China, and tried to take over Korea and Indo China. The Soviet government was behind all these "indirect aggressions" and now "Lebanon was selected to become a victim." He reminded his audience of the Eisenhower Doctrine, and said he was sending troops to Lebanon to protect Americans in that country and to preserve the territorial integrity and political independence of a nation under attack by communism. He asserted that the full Lebanese cabinet supported this request, although he knew the Lebanese army commander did not. He praised UN Secretary General Dag Hammarskjold for sending UNOGIL to Lebanon, which had substantially reduced cross-border arms infiltration. Chamoun, the president stressed, "does not seek reelection."[5]

The president closed by raising a familiar metaphor. "In the 1930's the members of the League of Nations became indifferent to direct and indirect aggression in Europe, Asia and Africa. The result was to make World War II inevitable." He promised "that history shall not now be repeated" and he hoped American troops "can be promptly withdrawn."[6]

It is a curious statement, both for what it says and, even more, for what it does not say. The references to communist indirect aggression were vintage 1950s American Cold War principals. No American leader wanted to be the next politician who had "lost" China or Czechoslovakia to international communism. So, the Soviet menace that Americans understood had to be found at the root of Lebanon's civil war. The disputed elections that Chamoun had engineered were judged free and fair, Chamoun's desire for a second term was flatly ignored, and the complexity of Lebanon's intricate politics was left unstated. Instead of referring to Eisenhower's real concern, Nasser's pursuit of Arab unity, the president turned the issue into avoiding another Munich-appeasing communist aggression and preventing World War III. It was a less than candid explanation for why the president and his cabinet felt they had to do "something."

Beirut Carnage Averted by Diplomacy

On the ground, Beirut was ripe for disaster on July 15, 1958. Eisenhower did not control the situation in the capital. Lebanese Muslims believed the U.S. intervention was against them and their struggle to oust Chamoun; Lebanese Christians believed the Americans were there to save them and keep Chamoun in power. Both were heavily armed and expecting a fight. The Lebanese army had not been informed by Chamoun, and its commander believed his duty was to defend his country against any aggressor.

The Americans were also expecting a fight and preparing for the worst. As standard procedure for going into combat, the European Command instructed an Honest John missile battery in Germany, equipped with missiles that used nuclear warheads, to deploy to Lebanon. The European Command headquarters informed the commanders on the ground in Beirut that they would send the missile battery by sea from Bremerhaven in Germany but airlift the nuclear warheads to ensure their safety. The commander of the Sixth Fleet countered and asked for the battery to come only with conventional warheads; he was informed it had no conventional warheads, only nuclear warheads. As soon as the battery arrived in Beirut, it was "returned to Germany by air immediately," according to the official military history of the operation.[7]

American diplomacy and cool heads prevented disaster that July. Two figures were critical: Ambassador to Lebanon Robert M. McClintock and Eisenhower's personal representative for Lebanon and deputy under secretary for political affairs in the State Department Robert Daniel Murphy. McClintock and Murphy were both professional diplomats with long service in the Department of State. McClintock, a Stanford University graduate, had been the first American ambassador to Cambodia before coming to Lebanon in January 1958. Murphy had decades of government service before Eisenhower summoned him to the White House on July 15 and made him the president's personal representative to the Middle East for the duration of the crisis. The two had worked together in Belgium when Murphy was ambassador and McClintock was head of the political section in the late 1940s and early 1950s.

McClintock was on the scene on July 15 and immediately understood the crucial importance of the Lebanese army commander General Fuad Chehab. Chamoun had not told Chehab that he was inviting the American landing, and Chehab tried to persuade McClintock not to let the Marines come ashore when he belatedly realized the invasion was imminent. He told the ambassador that the army was the only institution holding Lebanon together and if it collapsed Lebanon would be either "a Christian Israel or be inundated in the Sea of Islam."[8] McClintock worked closely with the American military commanders and Chehab to control the potentially fraught confrontation between the two commands.

The denouement came on the morning of July 16. The 5,000 Marines ashore began to move into the capital from their beachhead and the airport; a Marine battalion with six Patton tanks led the advance into the city. A Lebanese army detachment with tanks and artillery blocked the way with orders to open fire if the Marines advanced. Ambassador McClintock was meeting with Chamoun and Chehab at the presidential palace, where Chamoun demanded the Marines save him from the opposition and Chehab expressed his fear that the army would split apart. He told the ambassador that Lebanon was "on the brink of disaster."[9] When news of the armed confrontation arrived, McClintock and Chehab left to go to the site.

McClintock, Chehab, and U.S. Navy Admiral James Holloway, the newly appointed commander of the landing force, who had just arrived from London that morning, came together to the tense standoff. They agreed they would escort the Marines into Beirut by driving together in a civilian car at the head of the Marine column, creating the fiction that the Marines were the guests of the Lebanese army. It worked, and the immediate crisis was defused.[10] After July 16, the Marines were escorted whenever they went into Beirut, and even then they traveled only in small numbers. They did not enter areas controlled by the opposition United National Front. When by accident, on July 17, two Marines in a jeep got lost and wandered into the Basta, the Muslims captured them and took their weapons; they returned the Marines after a few hours via the army. If not for the "particularly high order of political vision demonstrated by the American ambassador, there is little doubt that American and Lebanese troops would have clashed and the landing turned into a political disaster," according to the foremost Lebanese account of the operation.[11] As McClintock later wrote, it was a "near miss."[12]

The Americans also took steps to keep the French, the former colonial power, from intervening. Charles de Gaulle had just come to power in Paris in June, and it was unknown how far he might go to reassert French influence in Lebanon. Holloway, a World War II, Korea, and Vietnam veteran, who would go on to become the chief of naval operations in the 1970s, persuaded the French, who had sent the cruiser *De Grasse* and several destroyers to the area, to make only a token visit to Beirut harbor on the evening of July 17 and to depart before the sun came up the next day.[13]

Murphy arrived after the initial confrontation had been smartly avoided by McClintock, Holloway, and Chehab. There was some concern in Washington that McClintock was too accommodating to Chamoun's enemies and less than fully supportive of the intervention. It was true that he had not thought the intervention was warranted on July 14. "The joke around Beirut was that Murphy's assignment was to prevent a coup within the U.S. Embassy," was how one CIA officer characterized the situation.[14]

In his memoirs, Murphy describes the evolution of his own thinking. In his first meeting with Chamoun, who had been surrounded in his residence for sixty-seven days as a "self-made prisoner," Murphy was outraged to hear that Chehab would not "clean out the Basta" and restore order. He thought Chehab should be fired. The capital was the most "trigger happy" place Murphy had seen since Berlin in 1945: "Wild fusillades, bombings and arson were the order of the day and more especially the night."[15]

But Murphy quickly began to change his mind, influenced by McClintock, Holloway, and Bill Eddy, a Lebanese American retired Marine who had been instrumental in setting up the American relationship with Saudi Arabia in World War II. Like the ambassador and the admiral, Eddy thought the root of the problem in Lebanon was Chamoun's ambition to have a second term as president. If he was replaced, the opposition would give up the civil war. Eddy helped arrange a series of meetings for Murphy with the opposition leadership. The first was with the former prime minister Saeb Salaam in the Basta. Eddy asked Salaam's deputy to order their men to cease sniping at the Marines "who were being shot at every night," and the shooting measurably calmed down. Another meeting followed with Kamal Junblatt in his stronghold in the Shuf mountains. Murphy and McClintock assured the Druze leader that the Marines were not in Lebanon to help the Christians or to keep Chamoun in power. Junblatt agreed to support an early presidential election and end the civil war. Finally, the American diplomats traveled to Tripoli to meet Rashid Karami, a future prime minister. Eddy was crucial in setting up all these sessions with the Muslim opposition and for setting the stage for a peaceful outcome.[16]

The next task was to find an acceptable candidate to replace Chamoun. Chamoun lobbied Murphy against General Chehab, but the American team believed the army commander was the best choice for the job. He alone could reach out to both sides as a neutral party. A graduate of the French military academy at St. Cyr, he was urbane and sophisticated, and he already had proven himself to the Americans by defusing the crisis on July 16.

On July 31, Chehab was elected president by a vote of 48 to 8 in parliament. Murphy left Beirut shortly before the vote to lower the American hand in the outcome. He later wrote, "Chehab had a vast amount of common sense and he accepted the office of President only as a compromise essential to peace in Lebanon."[17] The American intervention had been requested by Chamoun but ended in his replacement by the man Chamoun most disliked. American diplomacy had come to terms with local reality.

Murphy's key stop was Cairo. Nasser had been in Yugoslavia when the coup occurred in Iraq. He immediately put the UAR's armed forces on high alert and recognized the new government in Baghdad. Nasser had planned to return to Cairo on July 14 by sea in the Egyptian presidential yacht, but the Yugoslavs were concerned about Nasser's safety at sea in the midst of a regional crisis. Despite that, Nasser embarked to go home, and Soviet leader Nikita Khrushchev sent a plane to bring Nasser to Moscow on July 16. Nasser returned to port in Yugoslavia after getting the Russian message, and the Egyptian president secretly flew to Moscow to consult with the Soviets.

Recently declassified Soviet documents show that neither Khrushchev nor Nasser had anticipated the coup or had any role in it. In fact, Nasser told the Russians that he had no information about Qassem. The Russians had information from the Iraqi Communist Party that Qassem was opposed to the monarchy, but they had no direct interaction with him before the coup. On July 17, Khruschev and Nasser agreed to show resolve to defend the Iraqi coup but to avoid any involvement in resisting the Americans in Beirut. Both agreed that the Iraqi coup was the most important issue in the region; Beirut was a sideshow.[18]

The Soviets were concerned that Ike would intervene in Iraq. They accurately assessed that Vice President Richard Nixon was the most hawkish of Eisenhower's advisors. In fact, Nixon was the only one of Ike's advisors to even raise the idea of using military force in Iraq; Eisenhower never seriously considered the idea, and the military was against it as far too ambitious. The Russians sent a back-channel message to the administration using a Russian intelligence officer who posed as a journalist but was known to the FBI to be a member of Russian military intelligence, the GRU. At a lunch meeting with a Nixon aide in Georgetown, the GRU officer told the aide that an American intervention in Iraq would lead to a much larger war. The threat was unnecessary; Ike was not interested in putting American boots on the ground in Baghdad.[19]

The Egyptian media remained focused on Iraq and the downfall of Nasser's main rival, Nuri Sa'ed and the Hashemite monarchy. Iraq was the big game changer.

On July 18, 1958, Nasser surprised everyone by flying from Moscow to Damascus to demonstrate his support for Syria. He had been widely expected to travel to Baghdad.

Nasser had, in fact, requested permission to land in the Iraqi capital, but Qassem had turned him down. "It was a stunning rebuff for Nasser."[20] Qassem sent his deputy, Abdel Salam Arif, to Damascus instead, well aware that Arif was pro-Nasser. It was an early sign that the Iraqis were not going to follow Nasser. Qassem was his own man.

Murphy arrived in Egypt at Nasser's invitation after short stops in Jordan, Israel, and Iraq. Nasser received him in his residence and gave a five-hour monologue that went on until two in the morning. Nasser said he was pleased that Chamoun was gone and Chehab had become president. "He made voluble protestations of his desire to support the independence of Lebanon now that the hostile Chamoun propaganda machine would cease to function." He also attempted to assure Murphy, less convincingly, that the UAR was not seeking to oust King Hussein. The Egyptians and Americans remained at odds but not any longer over the presidency of Lebanon.[21] Nasser met with Chehab after his election in the border town of Chtourah and officially welcomed his presidency. Nasser instructed his lieutenants to cease all military support to the rebels.[22]

Saving King Hussein

While Beirut hovered on the brink of disaster in the first hours after the Marines landed, Amman was actually the most at-risk Western ally in the region. The king was the surviving member of the Hashemites and claiming to be the king of the Arab Federation. He was distraught at the murder of his family. On July 16, 1958, the British and American charges in Amman (technically still a part of the federation, so not ambassadors) were summoned to the palace. The king said he had more intelligence suggesting a coup plot was imminent, maybe even on the 17th, and therefore, he was requesting immediate military assistance by both Great Britain and the United States. The two diplomats responded that it would be the British military, given the division of labor already agreed to by Eisenhower and MacMillan. The British forces would deploy to the airport and royal palace; they would not enter the rest of Jordan unless attacked and would not be part of any intervention in Iraq. Their mission would be to protect the king and British citizens in Jordan, and by their presence try to stabilize the country. The United States would provide fuel and logistical support, essential in a country with no oil.[23]

The next day, July 17, a battalion of the British 16th Parachute Brigade was airlifted from Cyprus, still a British colony, to Amman. Ultimately 3,500 British troops were deployed to Jordan, along with a fighter squadron from the Royal Air Force. British forces in Libya, Aden, Bahrain, and Kuwait were also reinforced. MacMillan had closely consulted with Eisenhower to ensure smooth cooperation. The mission was called Operation Fortitude.[24]

America's two closest allies in the Middle East did nothing to assist Fortitude; in fact, they made the mission more difficult. As the first British airlift crossed Israeli territory to fly from Larnaca to Amman, the Israelis denied clearance and fired on the aircraft, forcing some planes to turn around and return to Cyprus. The Israelis claimed the British had provided insufficient advance warning. The American ambassador in Tel Aviv hurriedly met with Prime Minister Ben-Gurion and arranged clearance only after Washington promised to aid Israel in the event of "retaliatory action from any quarter." For the rest of Operation Fortitude, air clearance over Israel was a constant friction between the British and Americans and the Israelis. As the U.S. Air Force began conducting a large airlift of fuel to Amman, it was a low moment in America's relationship with Israel. By the end of July, the USAF had lifted over 1,500 tons of cargo to Jordan essential to the British mission and the economy of Jordan.[25]

The British assumed the Israelis were actually hoping for Hussein to fall from power, which would allow them the chance to seize East Jerusalem and the West Bank. The Americans worried about the same and told London that "the presence of British troops in Amman will not deter" Israel from taking the West Bank.[26] The Israelis pressed the Americans not only for a security guarantee but also for opening an arms supply, as Avi Shalem, an Israeli scholar, has written: "Israel's behavior in Jordan's hour of need was erratic and unhelpful . . . Israel sought a ludicrously high price for the privilege of using its airspace."[27]

Saudi Arabia was even more difficult. The nearest source of oil to supply Jordan and the British was in the Persian Gulf. The first shipment planned to lift to Amman was scheduled to fly from the American base in Dhahran, Saudi Arabia, but the Saudis refused to give overflight clearance.[28] Crown Prince Faisal, who had sidelined his brother Saud over the botched Syrian coup plot, made the decision. Hussein called Saud to appeal for help, but Saud said the issue was out of his hands. It was a "particularly bitter blow" for Hussein.[29]

Murphy did not include Riyadh in his mission to the region. The American ambassador met with Faisal on July 24 and "listened to an almost unadulterated Nasserian exposition of the situation in the Arab world." The crown prince said the Kingdom was opposed to any foreign military interference in the region and said "unwise people stir the fire and wise people get burned." The ambassador concluded that Faisal was buying time to "defer any Egyptian plot to overthrow the present Saudi regime."[30]

Faisal did travel to Cairo in August to see Nasser. CIA director Allen Dulles told Eisenhower that the crown prince was a "wily character" who was appearing to accommodate the Egyptians to "save the Saudi dynasty."[31] A SNIE commissioned by Dulles concluded that Faisal would pursue accommodation with the UAR to fend off "the already heavy pressures upon the Saudi dynasty."[32] Faisal did not reconcile with Hussein until the early 1960s.

Abandoned by his neighbors and distraught at his personal loss, Hussein went into seclusion for almost a week. His position was humiliating. He had sought to free Jordan from British control, ousting Glubb Pasha, but now was dependent on British soldiers to survive. The American airlift was keeping the country alive, but the American embassy reported to Eisenhower that he had the support of only 10 percent to 20 percent of the people. In August, Washington ordered all dependents to leave the country.[33] Hussein snapped back from his gloom and toured the country, rallying his Bedouin support base and the army.

Nasser helped the king in the end. The UN adopted a resolution sponsored by the Arab League calling for all states to observe "strict non-interference in each other's internal affairs." Hammarskjold came to Amman in late August; Hussein agreed to the establishment of a UN observer mission in Jordan, and Nasser embraced the mission. In October, Hussein announced the British paratroopers would leave, and they completed their withdrawal by November 2.[34]

Beirut and Baghdad

The Americans were also withdrawing as the political situation in Beirut calmed down. Fuad Chehab initially proposed a government "entirely of men from the opposition" to Chamoun, with Rashid Karami as prime minister. This provoked unrest from the Christians. Chehab orchestrated a reconciliation between Karami and the Phalangist militia boss Pierre Jumayyil in early October. A new cabinet was created with Karami as prime minister and Jumayyil as minister of public works and education. The policy of the government was "no victor, no vanquished," a formula invented by the Christian Phalangist leader. Immediately the country began to return to normal; barricades were removed and commercial activity resumed.[35]

The Marines and the Army began drawing down forces in September from a peak strength of 14,000. The Christians protested vocally their withdrawal while the Muslim opposition rejoiced. With the cabinet compromise, all sides quieted down. The last American soldier departed on October 25 after 102 days of Operation Blue Bat. The intervention cost the U.S. government $200 million dollars.[36]

Only one American serviceman, an army sergeant, died in combat; Sergeant James R. Nettles was shot by a sniper on August 2, 1958. He was the first American soldier to die in America's wars in the Middle East. No Lebanese suffered any injury as a result of U.S. military action.[37]

In retrospect, Miles Copeland, the CIA operative, wrote "the outcome was exactly what Gamal Abd al Nasser was seeking. It was as though the Marines had been brought in to achieve Nasser's objectives for him." Nasser had wanted Chamoun replaced with Chebab, and Karami as prime minister.[38] Chamoun, too, in retrospect, said that the Americans, particularly McClintock, had abandoned him in 1958.[39] In truth, American diplomacy had recognized reality, dealt with it effectively, and prevented what could have been a disaster. It was, as Copeland wrote, a "brilliant feat" by McClintock.[40]

The bloody coup in Iraq was the cause of the American intervention in Lebanon and the British in Jordan. All eyes were on Baghdad in the summer of 1958. Ambassador Waldemar J. Gallman was invited on July 15, 1958, to meet with General Abd al Karim Qassem. Qassem was fluent in English, and no translator was required. He said, "we Iraqis want to be friends with the U.S." He also assured the ambassador that U.S. citizens in Iraq would be safe and could be evacuated if they wanted. On returning to the embassy, Gallman learned Nuri al Saed had been hung and his body desecrated. He wrote that it was "tragically ironic that on the very day landing [was] made from the Sixth Fleet, which Nuri had so long pleaded for, Nuri was put to death."[41] Gallman had served four years in Baghdad before the coup and later wrote a very flattering book about Nuri.[42]

Qassem's words of friendship did not convince Washington. Iraq resumed diplomatic relations with the Soviet Union, broken in 1955, and opened relations with communist China. King Faisal Street in Baghdad was renamed Gamal Abd al Nasser Street. On July 19, an Iraqi delegation traveled to Damascus to meet with Nasser; the trip produced a mutual aid pact between the new Republic of Iraq and the UAR. Baghdad radio praised Nasser, and his photo was everywhere. The new government gave the impression that a merger with the UAR was imminent.[43] The mutual defense agreement, in particular, alarmed the State Department.[44]

In fact, however, Qassem was very much an Iraqi nationalist and more interested in revolution in Iraq than in unity with the rest of the Arab world. His focus was not on Cairo or Amman but on Baghdad. As the State Department later wrote, Qassem was "in strong contrast to Nasser an anti-imperialist devoid of the crusading spirit" of Arab unification. Qassem was not a "unity now" supporter; he was for Iraq first, which is why he refused to receive Nasser in Baghdad after the coup. This became apparent only over time.[45]

Murphy visited Baghdad before returning to Washington from the Middle East. The flight into Baghdad was harrowing; the Iraqis had provided flight clearance in advance but then ordered the aircraft to turn around once it entered Iraqi airspace. Murphy proceeded anyway and landed in a steamy 113-degree heat at the capital. Qassem met Murphy and Gallman at the Defense Ministry carrying a machine gun. Qassem stressed that the corrupt monarchy could be removed only by violence and did not deplore the brutality of the coup. But the Iraqi leader also stressed that the revolution was a national one, not part of a wider ideological cause.[46]

Qassem said he and his fellow officers were concerned that the Marine landing in Lebanon was only a prelude to an invasion of Iraq by the United States. Murphy responded that he had just flown over much of the country and he could see no reason "why Eisenhower would want to send American troops to invade the Godforsaken stretches of Iraq." Both Murphy and Qassem smiled at the joke. The Americans expressed concern at the large new Russian mission in Iraq. Qassem answered that he "had not risked revolution for the purpose of handing Iraq to the Soviet Union," adding that he and his associates also "had not risked their lives to make Iraq subservient to Egypt."[47] The fears of Allen Dulles were all wrong.

110

In September 1958, the leader of the Unity Now faction in the Iraqi regime, Abd al Salam Arif, who had led the attack into Baghdad in July, was demoted, from deputy commander of the armed forces to a position below Qassem. Shortly later, he was ousted from the cabinet and sent as ambassador to Germany. And on November 5, 1958, he was arrested for "plotting against the homeland." Though found guilty, he was not executed. The pro-Nasser faction of the Iraqi army was neutralized. Arif did not go away, but the danger of Iraq joining the UAR had passed.[48] In 1963, Qassem was ousted in a coup, and Arif became president. Arif then executed Qassem.

My family also departed the scene. Shortly after the Marines landed in Beirut, my mother, brother, and I were evacuated to Naples, Italy, where we were cared for at the Sixth Fleet headquarters of the U.S. Navy. My father remained in Lebanon with UNOGIL. We returned briefly to Lebanon in 1959 but came home to New York before the end of the year just in time to see the inauguration of John F. Kennedy.

Epilogue

LESSONS LEARNED

I returned to Beirut in 1985, twenty-seven years later, after the Marines were again sent ashore, this time by Ronald Reagan after Israel had launched its disastrous Operation Peace for Galilee in 1982. By 1985, the Marines barracks at the airport had been blown up, the embassy attacked twice, and the top CIA officer in the country kidnapped and murdered.

For security reasons, American diplomats traveled to the city by armed helicopter from Cyprus. The helicopter flew at twenty feet or so above the Mediterranean Sea to avoid radar, with machine guns deployed out the doors. The helicopter did not land; it just hovered over the landing zone at the embassy compound for two minutes while passengers jumped out or in. The embassy was a fortress, with a battalion of the Lebanese army surrounding it to stop suicide bombers. It was a sober insight into how American military operations in the Middle East had gone wrong.

There are four central lessons to be learned from studying our first combat mission in the Middle East. They are as useful today as they were in 1958 and in the years between.

First, don't panic. The Middle East is prone to surprise. Coups, revolutions, wars, and other developments arise suddenly and often with little or no warning. Or the warning is ignored, as happened in 2001 when the George W. Bush administration ignored the intelligence warnings that an al Qaeda attack was imminent. The mood in the White House when an unwelcome surprise comes from the Middle East is glum.

There is a natural temptation to do something. Eisenhower wrote about this "do something" attitude in his memoirs of July 1958. When the Iraqi coup occurred on July 14 that year, he felt a need to do something. The temptation to act was reinforced by Allen Dulles's scary briefing on the prospects for the Middle East after the coup when he painted such a picture of universal doom for American interests. All our allies were on the precipice of collapse, Dulles said, and Nasser was on the eve of taking over the entire Arab world. America could not afford to do nothing; it must act somewhere.

The better approach would have been to wait and see. The Marines were not needed on July 15, 1958, as Am-

*The author with his mother
and dog in Beirut.*

bassador McClintock had told the White House. Chamoun wanted them not because of Iraq but to extend his own time in office. McClintock's healthy skepticism about Chamoun was warranted, but the president and his team paid no attention because the events in Iraq had panicked them.

George H. W. Bush was also confronted by the unexpected from Iraq in 1990. The intelligence community had warned that Iraq was preparing to invade Kuwait, but when it happened, Bush took several days to assess the implications. He asked his intelligence director for an assessment of the implications, which ultimately persuaded the president to send troops to defend Saudi Arabia. Then he paused and waited again to see if Iraq would back down. Only when Baghdad insisted on staying in Kuwait did Bush order military action and, even then, only for a limited goal: the liberation of Kuwait, not the occupation of Iraq.

Waiting to see how developments play out can be nerve-racking, but it is better than panicking and overreacting. Time usually delivers a more nuanced assessment of a sudden change than the first impression.

Second, don't mislead the American people and the Congress about why you are sending troops into harm's way. American men and women should never go to war believing they are doing so for a reason that is different from why the president is really acting. In 2003, Americans thought Iraq had been involved in the 2001 attacks on our country. George W. Bush made no serious effort to disabuse them of this misconception; indeed, he fueled it with inaccurate information about contacts between al Qaeda and Iraq. On top of that, he fed the American people and Congress a bogus story about a threatening Iraqi arsenal of weapons of mass destruction, which Bush also knew was greatly exaggerated.

Walter Boomer, a veteran of the Vietnam and Iraq wars, says the greatest lesson of both is simply "tell the truth." It is the only way to sustain popular and congressional support for a war effort once casualties begin to mount up.[1]

Eisenhower was guilty of deceit in 1958. His address

to the nation as the Marines went ashore spoke about the danger of international communism in Iraq and Lebanon when no such danger existed. He conflated Arab nationalism and Moscow-directed communism as one and the same when they were very much different. Senator John F. Kennedy said so at the time. His own ambassador in Iraq said Moscow had "no hand" in the coup that startled Eisenhower into acting precipitously.[2]

The president also drew a false analogy, suggesting that if he did not act in Lebanon because of events in Iraq it would be a repetition of the Munich appeasement of Adolf Hitler in 1938. Invoking the specter of Munich was sure to arouse the American public into supporting his decision to send troops into combat for the first time in the Middle East, but it was not justified by the events on the ground.

Third, be very careful in listening to your allies in the region. Eisenhower had good reason to be cautious in appraising the views of his allies in 1958. Only two years earlier, Britain, France, and Israel had lied to him about their conspiracy to invade Egypt and sought to conceal their plans from the president. Ike learned his lesson in 1956.

In 1958, he learned that two of America's allies in the region, Israel and Saudi Arabia, were not reliable supporters of a third, Jordan. Indeed, they did a great deal to make American and British support for King Hussein harder rather than easier. Both Israel and Saudi Arabia, it appears, preferred Hussein's removal so they could expand their territory at the expense of Jordan, but Eisenhower did not let them get away with it.

Today, Israel and Saudi Arabia are eager for the United States to take on Iran and overthrow the Islamic government of Iran. They have legitimate grievances about Iranian behavior, but they do not justify sending American troops into combat. Iran is largely abiding by the nuclear deal it signed with Barack Obama in 2015. It would be a mistake to listen to our two allies in this case.

Fourth, and finally, listen to your diplomats and spies on the ground. Eisenhower and Dulles should have listened to Miles Copeland's report from Cairo in June 1958 that Nasser wanted to see Chehab replace Chamoun as president and that he harbored no ambition to seize Lebanon. Time proved Copeland's account was right.

Thankfully, Eisenhower did listen to Ambassador McClintock and his envoy Robert Murphy after the Marines went ashore in July. They counseled caution and avoiding a showdown with the Muslim opposition. Then they skillfully removed Chamoun from office and replaced him with Chehab, as Nasser had advocated. Thanks to them, the first Lebanese intervention did not end in a battle between American troops and Lebanese rebels backed by the rest of the Arab world. The diplomats, generals, and spies on the ground can get it wrong sometimes, of course; but generally as a rule their insights and advise are the best available.

In 1982, President Ronald Reagan ignored the advice of many of his diplomats in the region and the intelligence community in, first, supporting Israel's invasion of Lebanon (which was sparked by an Iraqi assassination attempt on the Israeli ambassador in London) and then panicking when the invasion bogged down. When disaster followed and Israeli-backed Phalangist militiamen massacred Palestinians in two refugee camps, Reagan sent in the Marines, supposedly as peace keepers. The administration was warned that they were at grave risk, but Reagan ignored the warnings and disaster ensued for the Marines at Beirut International Airport. The second time in Lebanon, twenty-five years after 1958, was a debacle.

Paying attention to these four lessons is a good way to avoid further debacles. The Middle East will be full of surprises for decades to come. America needs to react prudently and rationally. It should take its time to evaluate unexpected situations, avoid misleading its own public about its actions, be skeptical about its allies' intentions, and listen to its own experts when they council diplomacy instead of combat.

Notes

Chapter One

1. Avi Shlaim, *Lion of Jordan: The Life of King Hussein in War and Peace* (New York: Knopf, 2008), p. 86.

2. Uriel Dann, *King Hussein and the Challenge of Arab Radicalism, Jordan 1955–1967* (Oxford University Press, 1989), pp. 26–27.

3. Ray Takeyh, *The Origins of the Eisenhower Doctrine: The U.S., Britain and Nasser's Egypt, 1953–57* (New York: St. Martin's Press, Inc, 2000), p. 94.

4. Dann, p. 28.

5. Shlaim, p. 91.

6. Dann, pp. 29–30.

7. "Jordan at Risk," *The Times*, London, January 11, 1953. See also Dann, p. 30.

8. Nigel Ashton, *King Hussein of Jordan: A Political Life* (Yale University Press, 2008), pp. 49–50. See also Takeyh, p. 95.

9. Shlaim, pp. 93–94.

10. Nasser was the subject of numerous biographies during his life, but since his death there has been a dearth of biographical re-

search until Fawaz Gerges's *Making the Arab World: Nasser, Qutb, and the Clash that Shaped the Middle East* (Princeton University Press, 2018), which I have drawn from extensively.

11. Joel Gordon, *Nasser: Hero of the Arab Nation* (Oxford, One World, 2006), p. 26.

12. Gerges, p. 171.

13. Hugh Wilford, *America's Great Fame: The CIA's Secret Arabists and the Shaping of the Modern Middle East* (New York, Basic Books, 2013), p. 136. See also Stephen Ambrose, *Ike's Spies: Eisenhower and the Espionage Establishment* (New York, Anchor, 2012) and Evan Thomas, *The Very Best Men: The Daring Early Years of the CIA* (New York, Simon and Schuster, 2006).

14. David Kirkpatrick, *Into the Hands of Soldiers* (New York: Viking Press, 2018), p. 17.

15. Miles Copeland, *The Game of Nations: The Amorality of Power Politics* (London: Weidenfeld & Nicolson, 1969), pp. 51–53.

16. Wilford, p. 142.

17. Gerges, p. 174.

18. Max Hastings, *The Secret War: Spies, Ciphers and Guerrillas, 1939–1945* (New York: Harper Collins, 2016), pp. 303-31.

19. Takeyh, p. 43.

20. Wilford, pp. 146–47, 159.

21. Stephen Kinzer, *The Brothers: John Foster Dulles, Allen Dulles, and Their Secret World War* (New York: Henry Holt and Company, 2013), p. 211.

22. Wilford, pp. 155–57.

23. Gordon, pp. 42–43.

24. Alex Von Tunzelmann, *Blood and Sand: Suez, Hungary, and Eisenhower's Campaign for Peace* (New York: Harper, 2016), p. 95. Ms. Tunzelmann's book is the best new account of the 1956 crisis.

25. Tunzelmann, p. 98.

26. Wilford, p. 192.

27. Ibid., p. 176.

28. Benny Morris, *The Road to Jerusalem: Glubb Pasha, Palestine and the Jews* (London: I. B. Tauris, 2002), p. 231.

29. Morris, p. 237.

30. William I. Hitchcock, *The Age of Eisenhower: America and*

the World in the 1950s (New York: Simon and Schuster, 2018, pp. 306–07.

31. Tunzelmann, pp. 175–77.

32. Hitchcock, pp. 309–11.

33. "Exchange of Letters Bulganin-Ben Gurion," November 5 and 8, 1956, Ministry of Foreign Affairs, Israel.

34. Hitchcock, p. 118.

35. Ibid., p. 344. Also, Bruce Riedel, *JFK's Forgotten Crisis: Tibet, the CIA, and the Sino-Indian War* (Washington, DC: Brookings Institution Press, 2016), pp. 9–10.

36. Takeyh, pp. 150–51.

37. Dwight David Eisenhower, Eisenhower Doctrine Speech to Congress, January 5, 1957.

38. Ibid.

39. Ibid.

40. Hitchcock, p. 340.

Chapter Two

1. Kermit Roosevelt, *Countercoup: The Struggle for the Control of Iran* (New York: McGraw Hill, 1979). There are many books on the 1953 coup. See Mark Gasiorowski and Malcolm Byrne, editors, *Mohammad Mosaddeq and the 1953 Coup in Iran (Modern Intellectual and Political History of the Middle East)* (Syracuse University Press, 2017).

2. Patrick Seale, *The Struggle for Arab Independence: Riad el Solh and the Makers of the Modern Middle East* (Cambridge University Press, 2010), p. 582.

3. Douglas Little, "Cold War and Covert Action: The United States and Syria, 1945–1958," *Middle East Journal* 44, no. 1, Winter 1990, p. 55.

4. Little, p. 61.

5. Ibid., p. 63.

6. Ibid., pp. 65–67.

7. Dwight David Eisenhower, *Waging Peace: The White House Years, A Personal Account, 1956–1961* (New York: Doubleday, 1965), pp. 197–99.

8. Patrick Seale, *The Struggle for Syria: A Study of Post-War*

Arab Politics, 1945–1958 (Oxford University Press, 1965), pp. 303–06.

9. Parker T. Hart, *Saudi Arabia and the United States: Birth of a Security Partnership* (Indiana University Press, 1998), p. 113.

10. William T. Hitchcock, *The Age of Eisenhower: America and the World in the 1950s* (New York: Simon and Shuster, 2018), p. 438.

11. Waldemar J. Gallman, *Iraq Under General Nuri: My Recollections of Nuri al Said, 1954–1958* (Baltimore: Johns Hopkins University Press, 1964), p. 153.

12. Hart, p. 68.

13. Ibid.

14. Office of the Historian, Department of State, "Telegram from the Department of State to the Embassy in Saudi Arabia," March 3, 1958, *Foreign Relations of the United States, 1958–1960*, Near East Region; Iraq; Iran; Arabian Peninsula, Volume XII, Number 306.

15. Ibid., no. 306.

16. Eisenhower, *Waging Peace*, p. 264.

17. Alexei Vassiliev, *King Faisal of Saudi Arabia: Personality, Faith and Times* (London: Saqi Books, 2012), p. 214.

18. *FRUS*, Volume XII, Editorial Note, Number 307.

19. Ibid., "Telegram from the Department of State to the Embassy in Saudi Arabia," Number 309.

20. Vassiliev, *King Faisal*, p. 216.

21. *FRUS*, Volume XII, Editorial Note, Number 313.

22. Ibid., Special National Intelligence Estimate, SNIE 30-1-58, no. 315.

23. Ibid.

24. Ibid.

25. Ibid., no. 316.

Chapter Three

1. Patrick Seale, *The Struggle for Arab Independence: Riad el Solh and the Makers of the Modern Middle East* (Cambridge University Press, 2010), p. 321.

2. Ibid., p. 367.

3. Fouad Ajami and Eli Reed, *Beirut: City of Regrets* (New York: Norton, 1988), p. 21.

4. Benny Morris, *The Road to Jerusalem: Glubb Pasha, Palestine and the Jews* (London: I. B. Taurus, 2002), p. 148. See also Seale, p. 648.

5. Fahim I. Qubain, *Crisis in Lebanon* (Washington, DC: The Middle East Institute, 1961), p. 37.

6. Ibid., p. 38.

7. Ibid., p. 58.

8. Ajami and Reed, p. 26.

9. Qubain, pp. 8, 65.

10. Ibid., p. 63.

11. Ibid., p. 68.

12. Robert Murphy, *Diplomat Among Warriors* (New York: Doubleday, 1964), p. 401.

13. Qubain, p. 84.

14. Benny Morris, "Israel and the Lebanese Phalange: The Birth of a Relationship, 1948–1951," *Studies in Zionism* 5, no. 1 (1984), pp. 125–44.

15. Miles Copeland, *The Game of Nations: The Amorality of Power Politics* (London: Weidenfeld & Nicolson, 1969), p. 201.

16. Avi Shlaim, *Collusion Across the Jordan: King Abdullah, the Zionist Movement, and the Partition of Palestine* (Columbia University Press, 1988), p. 402.

17. Seale, pp. 716–17, 722, 725–27.

18. Avi Shlaim, *Lion of Jordan: The Life of King Hussein in War and Peace* (New York: Knopf, 2008), p. 46.

19. Shlaim, *Collusion Across the Jordan*, pp. 605–06.

20. Richard Cavendish, "A Failed Coup in Jordan," *History Today* 57, no. 4, April 2007.

21. Lawrence Tal, "Britain and the Jordan Crisis of 1958," *Middle Eastern Studies* 31, no. 1 (January 1995), p. 42.

22. Jack O'Connell, *King's Counsel: A Memoir of War, Espionage, and Diplomacy in the Middle East* (New York: Norton, 2011), p. 6.

23. See also Nigel Ashton, *King Hussein of Jordan: A Political Life* (Yale University Press, 2008), p. 72, and Uriel Dann, *King Hussein and the Challenge of Arab Radicalism, 1955–1957* (Oxford University Press, 1989), pp. 86–87. Dann credits Israel incorrectly for providing the intelligence on the 1958 plot.

24. Lawrence Tal, "Britain and the Jordan Crisis of 1958," *Middle Eastern Studies* 31, no. 1 (January 1995), p. 43.

Chapter Four

1. Interview with John, January 11, 2018.

2. Percy Cradock, *Know Your Enemy: How the Joint Intelligence Committee Saw the World* (London: John Murray, 2002), p. 131.

3. Christopher Catherwood, *Churchill's Folly: How Winston Churchill Created Modern Iraq* (New York: Basic Books, 2014).

4. Gerald de Gaury, *Three Kings in Baghdad: The Tragedy of Iraq's Monarchy* (London: I. B. Tauris, 2008), p. 2.

5. Uriel Dann, *Iraq Under Qassem: A Political History, 1958–1963* (New York: Praeger, 1969), p. 4.

6. Avi Shlaim, *Lion of Jordan: The Life of King Hussein in War and Peace* (New York: Alfred A. Knopf, 2008), pp. 157–58.

7. Elizabeth Monroe, *Britain's Moment in the Middle East, 1914–1956* (London: Meuthen and Company, 1963), p. 210.

8. Waldemar J. Gallman, *Iraq Under General Nuri: My Recollections of Nuri al Said, 1954–1958* (Baltimore: Johns Hopkins University Press, 1964), p. 150.

9. Shlaim, pp. 157–59.

10. Dann, p. 20.

11. Ibid., pp. 21–22.

12. Shlaim, p. 161.

13. de Gaury, p. 188.

14. Dann, pp. 28–31.

15. Monroe, p. 210.

16. Dann, p. 70.

17. Ibid., pp. 32–34.

18. Gallman, p. 181.

19. Office of the Historian, Department of State, Foreign Relations of the United States, 1958–1960, Near East Region; Iraq; Iran; Arabian Peninsula, Volume XII, "Telegram from the Embassy in Iraq to the Department of State," Baghdad, July 14, 1958, Document 112.

20. Shlaim, p. 167.

21. Ibid., pp. 163, 167.

22. Dwight D. Eisenhower, *Waging Peace: The White House Years, A Personal Account, 1956–1961* (New York: Doubleday Books, 1965), p. 269.

23. *FRUS*, Lebanon and Jordan, Volume XI, "Telegram from the Embassy in Lebanon to the Department of State," Beirut, July 14, 1958, Document 121.

24. Ibid., Document 125.

25. *FRUS*, Volume XII, "Briefing Notes by Director of Central Intelligence Dulles," Washington, DC, July 14, 1958, Document 110.

26. Ibid.

27. Ibid.

28. *FRUS*, Volume XI, "Memorandum of a Conference with the President, White House, Washington, DC, July 14, 1958, 10:50 a.m.," Document 124.

29. Robert D. Little and Wilhelmine Burch, *Air Operations in the Lebanon Crisis of 1958* (Washington, DC: United States Air Force Historical Division Liaison Office, October 1962, p. 10. Originally published as SECRET, declassified later to unclassified.

30. Eisenhower, *Waging Peace*, p. 272.

31. Stephen Kinzer, *The Brothers: John Foster Dulles, Allen Dulles, and Their Secret World War* (New York: Times Books, 2013), p. 243.

32. *FRUS*, Volume XII, "Telegram from the Embassy in Jordan to the Department of State," Amman, July 14, 1958, 3 p.m., Document 111.

33. *FRUS*, Volume XII, "Telegram from the Embassy in Israel to the Department of State," Tel Aviv, July 15, 1958, 1 a.m., Document 114.

34. *FRUS*, Volume XI, "Memorandum of Conversation, Department of State, Washington, DC, July 14, 1958," Document 129.

35. Alistair Horne, *Harold Macmillan, Volume II: 1957–1986* (New York: Penguin Books, 1989), p. 93.

36. *FRUS*, Volume XI, "Memorandum of a Telephone Conversation between President Eisenhower in Washington and Prime Minister Macmillan in London, July 14, 1958, 5:43 p.m.," Document 131.

37. Evan Thomas, *Ike's Bluff: President Eisenhower's Secret Battle to Save the World* (New York: Back Bay Books, 2012), p. 296.

Chapter Five

1. Richard D. Little and Wilhelmine Burch, *Air Operations in the Lebanon Crisis of 1958* (Washington, DC: United States Air Force Historical Division Liaison Office: October 1962), p. 24.

2. Dwight Eisenhower, *Waging Peace: The White House Years, A Personal Account, 1956–1961* (New York: Doubleday, 1965), pp. 275–78.

3. Evan Thomas, *Ike's Bluff: President Eisenhower's Secret Battle to Save the World* (New York: Back Bay Books, 2012), p. 15.

4. Dwight D. Eisenhower, "Statement by the President following the Landing of United States Marines at Beirut," The American Presidency Project, University of California, XXXIV President of the United States: 1953–1961, Document 173, July 15, 1958.

5. Ibid.

6. Ibid.

7. Little and Burch, p. 39. Eisenhower refers to the "Honest John rocket battery with atomic capability" deployment in his memoirs, *Waging Peace*, p. 286.

8. Little and Burch, p. 34.

9. Robert McClintock, "The American Landing in Lebanon," *U.S. Naval Institute Proceedings,* October 1962, p. 70.

10. Ibid, p. 37.

11. Fahim I. Qubain, *Crisis in Lebanon* (Washington, DC: The Middle East Institute, 1961), pp. 116–19.

12. McClintock, p. 71.

13. Ibid., p. 69.

14. Thomas W. Lippman, *Arabian Knight: Colonel Bill Eddy USMC and the Rise of American Power in the Middle East* (Vista, Calif.: Selwa Press, 2008), p. 284.

15. Robert Murphy, *Diplomat Among Warriors* (New York: Doubleday, 1964), p. 400.

16. Murphy, pp. 404–06, and Lippman, p. 284.

17. Murphy, p. 408.

18. Aleksander Fursenko and Timothy Naftali, *Khrushchev's Cold War* (New York: Norton, 2007), p. 78.

19. Ibid., p. 83.

20. Said K. Aburish, *Nasser: The Last Arab* (New York: St. Martin's Press, 2004), p. 172.

21. Murphy, pp. 410–11.

22. Aburish, p. 173.

23. Lawrence Tal, "Britain and the Jordan Crisis of 1958," *Middle Eastern Studies* 31, no. 1 (January 1995), p. 44.

24. Little and Burch, p. 54.

25. Ibid, p. 55.

26. Tal, p. 48.

27. Avi Shalem, *Lion of Jordan: The Life of King Hussein in War and Peace* (New York: Knopf, 2008), p. 165.

28. Little and Burch, p. 55.

29. Shalem, p. 166.

30. "Telegram from the Embassy in Saudi Arabia to the Department of State," *FRUS*, 1958–1960, Near East Region; Iraq; Iran; Arabian Peninsula, Volume XII, Jidda, July 25, 1958, Document 319.

31. Editorial Note, *FRUS*, Volume XII, Document 321.

32. Special National Intelligence Estimate, *FRUS*, Volume XII, September 9, 1958, SNIE 36.6-58, Document 322.

33. Tal, p. 49.

34. Ibid., pp. 49–50.

35. Qubain, p. 161.

36. Murphy, p. 408.

37. Qubain, p. 120.

38. Miles Copeland, *The Game of Nations: The Amorality of Power Politics* (London: Weidenfeld & Nicolson, 1969), p. 205.

39. Camille Chamoun, *Crise au Moyen-Orient* (Beirut: Editions Gallimaid, 1963), p. 11.

40. Copeland, p. 204.

41. "Telegram from the Embassy in Iraq to the Department of State," *FRUS*, Volume XII, Baghdad, July 15, 1958, Document 116.

42. Waldemar J. Gallman, *Iraq Under General Nuri: My Recollections of Nuri Al-Said, 1954–1958* (Baltimore: Johns Hopkins University Press, 1964).

43. Uriel Dann, *Iraq Under Qassem: A Political History, 1958–1963* (New York: Praeger, 1969), pp. 53, 70, and 73.

44. "Memorandum from the Director of Intelligence and Research (Cumming) to the Counselor (Reinhardt)," *FRUS*, Volume XII, Washington, DC, July 20, 1958, Document 126.

45. Ibid, p. 68.

46. Murphy, p. 413.

47. Ibid, p. 414.

48. Dann, pp. 80–85.

Epilogue

1. Max Hastings, *Vietnam: An Epic Tragedy, 1945–1975* (New York, Harper Collins, 2018), p. 746.

2. Waldemar J. Gallman, *Iraq Under General Nuri: My Recollections of Nuri al Said, 1954–1958* (Baltimore: Johns Hopkins University Press, 1964), p. 205.

Index